America's Financial Apocalypse and the Return of the Left

America's Financial Apocalypse and the Return of the Left

Fernando Meisenhalter

This book is intended for information and educational purposes only. The financial information contained in this book is not meant to supplement or replace proper training in finance, nor to give financial, or any other kind of advice. To obtain such advice, professionals must be consulted.

ISBN: 9781720273486

Imprint: Independently published

CONTENTS

1. A BIG SHIFT TO THE LEFT?

The United States will soon face a major shift to the Left. This may sound absurd today, with the country in the midst of an epic shift to the Right, with voters many times backing the most radical right-wing candidates they can find. According to a 2016 Gallup poll, a full third of the US now self-defined as *conservative*, and with only a minority (25%) self-defining as *liberal*. Liberal America, thus, seemed to barely be able to hold its own. But this was only part of the picture. America's fastest growing ideology today was the *liberal* ideology, with liberals here going from just 17% of the total population in 1992, to 25% in 2016, according to Gallup. This same Gallup study also pointed out that this rapid growth was "mainly at the expense of moderates," meaning rising liberals here were coming from America's center, and shifting moderates to the Left, not to the Right.[1] A 25% self-identification with liberal ideology might

---

[1] Also, "conservative views," for the first time in decades, showed a decline, although a small one, dropping from 36% in 2008, to 34% in 2016. For more data, see: *http://news.gallup.com/poll/201152/conservative-liberal-gap-continues-narrow-tuesday.aspx*

seem paltry. But many causes by American *conservatives* were actually more liberal than rightwing. Almost all Americans (84%), including many conservatives, for instance, supported background checks for gun buyers. And more than half (66%) were in favor raising the federal minimum wage. And more than half again (60%) believed that "it is the federal government's responsibility to make sure all Americans have healthcare coverage." Finally, another half (58%) believed abortion should be legal in all or most cases;[2] all liberal causes, even when, in many times, so many voters labelled themselves *conservatives*.[3]

Party preference between Republicans and Democrats in America was also "essentially tied" for the past half a century. But starting in 2019, polls now showed Republican preference falling well below half of all US voters, to just 39%,[4] with the US here undergoing what Gallup called a "dramatic" shift in favor of Democrats.[5] Party preference can be fickle, and vary over time, but "Democrats have held an edge in most years" since at least 1991, Gallup found, even setting the stage for liberals to grow "nationally in future years."[6]

Also, the number of Democrats in Congress that now

---

[2] *http://prospect.org/article/most-americans-are-liberal-even-if-they-don%E2%80%99t-know-it*

[3] *https://fivethirtyeight.com/features/the-moderate-middle-is-a-myth/*

[4] *https://www.wsj.com/articles/voters-increasingly-favor-democrats-for-congress-new-poll-shows-1513519201*
Democrats gained 26 percentage points in party preference here. "Republican margins were substantially smaller in [rural]... areas, going from a 35-point advantage for Republicans in 2016 down to 28 points this year [2018]." See: *https://www.catalist.us/news-innovation/2018-news/what-happened-last-tuesday-part-2who-did-they-vote/*

[5] *https://news.gallup.com/poll/315734/party-preferences-swung-sharply-toward-democrats.aspx*

[6] *This was going from just 25% in 1994; to 40% in 2010; to 50% in 2017; and to 54% in 2022. https://news.gallup.com/poll/467897/party-preferences-evenly-split-2022-shift-gop.aspx*
https://news.gallup.com/poll/467888/democrats-identification-liberal-new-high.aspx

described themselves as *liberal* also grew to a majority for the first time since 2014. Just four years before that, less than a third had self-described as liberal, according to *Wall Street Journal* data.[7]

This seems to point at a shift Left that was clearly "structural," or long-term; or linked to fundamental changes such as age, education, occupation, ethnicity, gender, and income. Suburban voters, for instance, which, since the 1950s, had been *overwhelmingly* conservative, and the bedrock of the Republican presidents like Eisenhower, Nixon, Reagan, H.W. Bush, and W. Bush, had now, since 2016, began to break this half a century or so pattern, with suburbs now becoming 50-50 Democrat and Republican.[8] Why this structural change? Simple: *poverty*. America's suburbs were also growing poorer at a faster rate than the rest of the country. Between 2000 and 2015, for instance, poverty here exploded by a whopping 57%, while poverty on average had "only" grown by 20% in the US.[9] Poverty, it seemed, bred Democrats. Even in the suburbs.

Another structural change were "White voters *with* a college degree," usually Democrat-leaning, which had, *in relative terms*, doubled in number since 1976. Meanwhile, during this same time, right-wingers had *lost* ground. Since 1976, "White voters without a college degree," mostly Republican, had, in *relative* terms, shrunk by half. This "wrestling crowd," or, very inappropriately, "deplorables," had been the ones that carried Donald Trump to the White House in 2016 and in 2024. Yet, *relatively* speaking, they were now losing ground to younger

---

[7] *https://www.wsj.com/graphics/divisions-among-the-democrats/*
https://news.gallup.com/poll/201152/conservative-liberal-gap-continues-narrow-tuesday.aspx

[8] Each of the two major parties received a total of about 37 million votes in 2016.
https://www.nytimes.com/2019/10/25/us/democrats-republicans-suburbs.html
https://www.inquirer.com/politics/inq/pennsylvania-polarization-election-results-democrats-republicans-trends-map-20190207.html

[9] *https://www.brookings.edu/testimonies/the-changing-geography-of-us-poverty/*

generations, prompting *The New York Times* to argue that *time* "was not on President Trump's side," and that this voting base was losing ground with time.[10]

Many argued that Trump had still gotten a solid 46% of the popular vote back in 2016, and an absolute majority in 2024.[11] But again, this missed the *overall* picture.[12] Democrat Hillary Clinton had won a majority of the popular vote in 2016, and gotten almost three million votes more than Trump.[13] Trump's 2024 win, although broader, had still been built largely on left-leaning voters staying away from polls, in part due to the awful lackluster Democrat candidate Kamala Harris, and also due to the discouraging high inflation at the time, which doomed the incumbent Democrats, and further demoralized would-be left-leaning voters. Trump's win here was, thus, driven more "by a decline in Democratic votes... than [by] an increase in Republican ones."[14]

Young Americans

Another example of this left-leaning *structural* trend was America's younger generations. Those born between 1981 and 1995, or Millennials, for instance, were, from the get go, *overwhelmingly* left-leaning. Back in 2016, they favored the

---

[10] College degree and minority crowds add up to 61%, a big majority. Meanwhile, "white voters without college degrees" had fallen from 71% to 39% between 1976 and 2018. For complete set of data, see: *https://www.nytimes.com/interactive/2020/10/22/us/politics/trump-voters-demographics.html* Interestingly, more than three-quarters of the leftwing Occupy Wall Street protesters in New York City in 2011 were college graduates. *https://www.nytimes.com/2022/04/28/business/college-workers-starbucks-amazon-unions.html*

[11] *https://www.pewresearch.org/politics/2018/08/09/an-examination-of-the-2016-electorate-based-on-validated-voters/*

[12] Democrats got 48.2% of the vote, versus 46.1% for the Republicans. See: *https://www.270towin.com/2016_Election/*

[13] *https://abcnews.go.com/Politics/hillary-clinton-officially-wins-popular-vote-29-million/story?id=44354341*

[14] *https://nysfocus.com/2024/11/09/low-voter-turnout-trump-harris*

Democratic Socialist presidential hopeful Bernie Sanders, and by an absolutely massive margin of 80%. Millennials, in aggregate, in primaries and caucuses voted overwhelmingly for Sanders; and among those under 30, they voted for Sanders more than for Trump *and* Hillary Clinton *combined*.[15] No wonder the Press now began talking of a rise in the "appeal" of socialism, especially among these younger voters, "driven [especially] by Black Americans and women," as the *Axios* news website put it.[16] This generational shift even felt rooted in a *cultural* force, with Millennial pop star Taylor Swift, for instance, also backing liberal causes, including fourth-wave feminism, #blacklivesmatter, and the "de-coding of gender binaries."[17] Called a Millennial Bruce Springsteen, Swift was also a strong critic of Trump.[18]

Another sign of the left-tilting of Millennials was gun control. The 2018 shooting at Stoneman Douglas High School that left 17 dead, and 17 wounded, led to the "March for Our Lives" in some 800 towns and cities across the US, and to the mobilizing of hundreds of thousands of younger folk, making this march perhaps the first Millennial mass mobilization ever. It was, of course, organized mainly by their moms, and gun

---

[15] *https://www.washingtonpost.com/news/the-fix/wp/2016/06/20/more-young-people-voted-for-bernie-sanders-than-trump-and-clinton-combined-by-a-lot https://www.theguardian.com/world/2018/apr/15/us-protests-vietnam-war-parkland-shooting-young-people https://www.theatlantic.com/politics/archive/2016/02/the-liberal-millennial-revolution/470826/* Americans kept their positive image of Senator Sanders. As late as October 2018, Sanders still enjoyed 53% favorable opinion —more than President Trump, or, for that matter, Senator Hillary Clinton at that time. *https://news.gallup.com/poll/243539/americans-maintain-positive-view-bernie-sanders.aspx?*

[16] *https://www.axios.com/americas-continued-move-toward-socialism-84a0dda7-4b8d-483a-8c4e-0c2e562c4e67.html*

[17] *https://nationalpost.com/entertainment/music/what-taylor-swift-tells-us-about-future-generations*

[18] *https://www.refinery29.com/en-us/2020/01/9334171/taylor-swift-political-views-history-miss-americana*

control was not always central in many of the teen's minds here, as some data suggested.[19] But the feeling was still one of long-held liberal causes, including gun control.[20]

And the generation that came after the Millennials, the Gen Zs, or Zoomers —born after 1995—, were even *more* liberal. Zoomers were also shifting Left. And since 2019, Zoomers now made up 20% of the total US voting population; and according to a *New York Times* poll, the vast majority of them (70%) wanted the government to do *more* for the people, and not less —an opinion clearly opposite to the traditional push for a minimal government upheld by the Right.[21]

Zoomers also gave Democrat Joe Biden much voting power for his 2020 win as President. "Young voters backed Mr. Biden over Mr. Trump by 61% to 36%," the *Wall Street Journal* reported, citing this also as one of the main reasons for his win that year.[22]

Zoomers from *conservative* rural areas were also less likely to vote Republican than in prior generations. Support for Trump in rural areas, for instance, had actually dropped by a good half just between 2016 and 2018.[23] So, even rural

---

[19] *https://www.nationalreview.com/news/only-12-percent-of-first-time-protesters-at-march-for-our-lives-were-there-for-gun-control/*

[20] *https://www.npr.org/sections/thetwo-way/2018/03/24/596679790/hundreds-of-thousands-march-for-gun-control-across-the-u-s*
http://time.com/longform/never-again-movement/

[21] Only 30% of Gen Zs approved of President Trump. For more data, see: *https://www.nytimes.com/2019/01/23/us/gop-liberal-america-millennials.html* Zoomers also didn't seem to like individualism. Older generations supported individualists like the libertarians more, including Ayn Rand's novel Atlas Shrugged. Even the rightwing strategist Steve Bannon noticed it. He once asked, for instance: "Where's my copy of 'Atlas Shrugged'?'" And then he answered: "It's in the shredder." *https://www.courant.com/coronavirus/ct-nw-nyt-they-predicted-crisis-of-2020-20200528-uicilca37rbenk3tn7i5oqdk4q-story.html*

[22] *https://www.wsj.com/articles/young-voters-helped-biden-beat-trump-after-holding-back-in-primaries-11606399200*

[23] It went from a 17-point margin, to a mere 8-point one. For more data, see: *https://www.washingtonpost.com/politics/2020/06/06/floyd-protests-are-broadest-us-history-are-spreading-white-small-town-america/* Polls also found that the

America, one more traditional bastion of the Right, was now also shifting away from core conservative ideals.

One might feel tempted to dismiss such liberal trends found among Millennials and Zoomers as just youth's idealism. But demographers have found that such generational convictions do not necessarily wither with age. On the contrary, *conservative* Gen Z's were much more likely to remain moderate, even into old age, even becoming a "long-term threat" then to the future of the Republican Party. Demographers therefore were forecasting Zoomers to even "substantially" reshape America's future "political and economic landscape," with a shift here towards *moderation*, not a growing radicalism of the Right, as *The New York Times* reported.[24]

Only older Americans, such as the Silent Generation, or individuals born between 1928 and 1945, showed stronger Republican identification, at 39%. But since then, Republican identification has been falling with every new generation. And by the time the polls reach the Zoomers, only 17% here identified as Republican. It was true that younger generations also tended to cared less about the Democrat-Republican divide, and were, overall, "more politically independent than older generations." But still, Republican political "messaging" was only strong among older generations, to the point where "only about one in five adults" under 41 identified as Republican, as Gallup also found.[25]

Most "Republican and Republican-leaning registered voters"

---

younger a Republican, the more moderate she'll be, and a growing number of younger Republicans were now rapidly moderating in their political views, at least since 2021. *https://www.axios.com/americas-continued-move-toward-socialism-84a0dda7-4b8d-483a-8c4e-0c2e562c4e67.html*

[24] *https://www.nytimes.com/2019/01/23/us/gop-liberal-america-millennials.html*

[25] *https://news.gallup.com/poll/397241/millennials-gen-clinging-independent-party.aspx*

in 2020 (56%) were now 50 years or older. In contrast, most Democrats were younger, if only by a few years —but growing more so with time.[26] This could be seen in protests. Occupy Wall Street protesters, for instance, all left-leaning, had been, on average, 29 years old.[27] And Black Lives Matter protestors had been mostly in the mid-thirties, with more than a third being under 30.[28] In contrast, the rightwing protesters of the 2021 Capitol Attack had been, on average, 41 years old —more than ten years older than their liberal counterparts.[29]

Unions

Another sing of a structural shift towards the Left was the increasing support for Unions. In the past, America's Unions had done nothing but *lose* support among the public. Not anymore. After the 2008 Global Financial Crisis —the most serious such crisis since the 1930s—, support for Unions suddenly began to rise, reaching an incredibly high 71% by 2020 —higher even than the support seen here during the more liberal 1960s.[30] Why this sudden uptick? Perhaps it was the result of those ten million people losing their homes, jobs, and life savings during the 2008 crisis. Not surprisingly perhaps, the youth here was at the forefront of this rising pro-Union trend, with the *younger college-educated, generations* being the most supportive for Unions. Among younger college

---

[26] *https://www.pewresearch.org/politics/2020/06/02/the-changing-composition-of-the-electorate-and-partisan-coalitions/* Also, most independent voters in 2020 had "[broken] for democrats in the midterms," the *Wall Street Journal* said. *https://www.wsj.com/articles/why-independent-voters-broke-for-democrats-in-the-midterms-11668249002*

[27] *https://www.newyorker.com/news/john-cassidy/wall-street-protests-who-are-the-99-and-what-do-they-want*

[28] *https://www.pewresearch.org/fact-tank/2020/06/24/recent-protest-attendees-are-more-racially-and-ethnically-diverse-younger-than-americans-overall/*

[29] *https://www.cbsnews.com/news/capitol-riot-arrests-latest-2021-07-20/*

[30] *https://news.gallup.com/poll/398303/approval-labor-unions-highest-point-1965.aspx*

graduates, for instance, the percentage supporting Unions was among the highest in the country,[31] a trend that was now being dubbed by *The New York Times* as, "The Revolt of the College-Educated Working Class." According to the *Times* also, college-educated workers had been taking more frontline jobs in places like Starbucks and/or Amazon since 2008, thus driving support for Union elections by more than 50% by the early 2020s. College-educated Union leaders were also making unionization drives more multiracial and multi-ideological. As one leader here put it: "Amazon doesn't allow people of differing education levels to become separated. It was the way we were able to unite people —the idea that we're all getting screwed." He then concluded: "We had straight-up Communists and hard-line Trump supporters." And somehow it worked.[32] In fact, mobilization grew so much, and so strong, that the Press dubbed 2023 as the year of the Unions, with more than half a million workers having gone on strikes in this year alone, more than double the rate in prior years. Film and TV writers, for instance, went on strike here; as did the Screen Actors Guild (a combo not seen, by the way, since 1960). UPS Teamsters also went on strike, one of the largest in US history. The United Auto Workers also went on strike, and in all three major Detroit companies: Ford, GM, and Stellantis. President Biden even dropped by at the picket here, the first president ever to do so. That year, there was a strike also against Pennsylvania's WabTec locomotive plant, and one against healthcare giant Kaiser Permanente.[33] Even Wells Fargo employees were

---

[31] In fact, it was an almost 50-year record high, suggesting a return to levels not seen since the 1930s. *https://news.gallup.com/poll/265916/labor-day-turns-125-union-approval-near-year-high.aspx*

[32] *https://www.nytimes.com/2022/04/28/business/college-workers-starbucks-amazon-unions.html*

[33] *https://www.businessinsider.com/2023-year-of-the-strike-unions-sag-aftra-uaw-2023-12*

planning to hold elections to form a Union, which, if successful, would then be a first "at a major bank in decades," as the *Wall Street Journal* pointed out.[34] Workers at digital media outlets, think tanks, and nonprofit groups, were also complaining of low pay and long hours, and also starting to unionize.

Socialism

Yet one more sign of this *structural* shift to the Left might also be in the growing support for "socialism," especially among Blacks, the youth, and women, and among Democrats in general.

It's true Americans in general still favored capitalism more than socialism in 2021, at a rate of 60% against only 38%, a percentage that has stayed constant more or less since 2010. But it was equally true that, starting in 2018, socialism had now grained much more ground, at least among Democrats. Among Democrats in 2018, for instance, 62% now said they favored socialism, while only 52% had done so ten years earlier.[35]

It was also true that the Democratic Socialists of America saw a doubling of members between 2015 and 2020. But its membership here was still very small —ten times smaller than that of the far-right Libertarian Party, for instance. But socialists were growing more rapidly now than libertarians, perhaps indicating they were starting to catch up.[36]

This might also explain why socialists were winning more elections than ever before. Democratic Socialists, for instance,

---

[34] *https://www.wsj.com/finance/banking/two-wells-fargo-branches-vote-to-form-union-0595107c?mod=hp_lead_pos10*

[35] *https://news.gallup.com/poll/357755/socialism-capitalism-ratings-unchanged.aspx*

[36] In early 2020, it had 66,000 members, still low compared to the Libertarian party, which had 10 times that number. For a more complete study, see: *https://www.theatlantic.com/politics/archive/2020/05/dsa-growing-during-coronavirus/611599/ has 66 thousand members, and*

had won 35 seats in US state legislatures back in 2017. One victory, that of Lee Carter (a former Marine who suffered an industrial accident and had fallen through the cracks of the workman's compensation system), was notable in that he got elected as a socialist in the rather conservative Virginia state legislature.[37] Public attitudes towards socialism also seemed to be changing, with the candidates now seeking "to attack opponents" by calling them *socialists* finding out that this term was no longer "an all-purpose pejorative" as used before. In fact, *socialism* was increasingly worn now "as a badge of pride."[38]

Gallup even argued that the US, as a whole, was gaining a "more socialist orientation." Support for socialism, it said, rose from 53% to 57% in the eight years between 2010 and 2018, a slight change perhaps, but, interestingly, also a rise that happened at a time when support for capitalism had fallen rapidly, from 53% to just 47%, a minority now.[39] Even Trump's White House advisors were worried. Socialism, they said, was "making a comeback in American political discourse... gaining support in Congress and among much of the electorate."[40]

Another significant victory for socialism was the victory of Alexandria Ocasio-Cortez in 2018. A Democratic Socialist from New York City, she ran for the US Congress. But it wasn't just that she won, but *how* she won. She defeated a 10-term Democrat incumbent, Joe Crowley, a top Party "insider" —the

---

[37] He also favored single-payer healthcare (a form of socialized medicine), and challenged the existing anti-union laws ("right-to-work" laws) in the state of Virginia. *https://www.nytimes.com/2017/11/10/opinion/democrats-election-obama-coalition.html*

[38] *https://www.axios.com/americas-continued-move-toward-socialism-84a0dda7-4b8d-483a-8c4e-0c2e562c4e67.html*

[39] *https://news.gallup.com/poll/240725/democrats-positive-socialism-capitalism.aspx?*

[40] *https://www.theguardian.com/us-news/2018/oct/23/the-socialists-are-coming-white-house-sounds-alarm-at-rise-of-the-left*

chairperson, no less, of Congress' powerful Democratic Caucus. Ocasio-Cortez was unknown, and Crowley had been a favorite, and yet still lost, leading to a massive political upset. At just 28 years old, Ocasio-Cortez became the youngest Representative, yet one more sign of the growing influence of democratic socialism among America's youth, and especially among women.

Just two years later, another socialist, Marcela Mitaynes, beat one more powerful Democrat, 26-year incumbent in the New York State Assembly, an ultimate "insider." And just as with Ocasio-Cortez, Mitaynes won by sticking to core issues (housing and healthcare); relying on grassroots organization more than on the ways of more mainstream Democratic candidates, which was through insider endorsements and huge amounts of money.[41]

Yet one more electoral upset came from a 44 year-old middle school principal, Jamaal Bowman. Although not a socialist, he won a New York seat in the US Congress in 2020 after defeating one more long-time Democrat incumbent, Eliot Engel. (Engel was another powerful party "insider" operating *since the late 1980s*, and among the "most" powerful "inside players," in fact, in the Party at that time.) Bowman also won by sticking to core issues and grassroots organizing, just as Ocasio-Cortez and Marcela Mitaynes did. Bowman, it's true, benefited from the Black Lives Matter protests from that year, but his victory still fell into that overall pattern of outsider candidates shifting to the Left, and sticking to grassroots organizing, deifying the traditional machinery of the

---

[41] *https://www.brooklynpaper.com/breaking-democratic-socialist-wins-sunset-park-assembly-seat-26-year-incumbent-concedes/* As Ocasio-Cortez herself pointed out during the congressional elections of 2020: "every single swing seat member that co-sponsored Medicare For All won their re-election."
https://www.theguardian.com/us-news/2020/nov/08/alexandria-ocasio-cortez-ends-truce-by-warning-incompetent-democratic-party

Democratic Party.

Some might dismiss such relatively isolated wins as a fad for some minor "lefty insurgency." But one University of Pennsylvania expert, Daniel Gillion, disagreed, noticing that this also *structural*, backed by Democrats that were now "more mobilized, more likely to give, and more energized,"[42] and also willing to support "anti-establishment" figures, and challenging "insiders" on an ongoing basis, and, thus, not likely to be just some "lefty fad."[43]

One more example of the same: the *incumbent* Democrat, Edward Markey, turned "outsider," and then taking up core popular issues and grassroots organizing in the Massachusetts elections of 2020, and winning the endorsement of socialist Ocasio-Cortez. His challenger, Joe Kennedy III —the grandson of the brother of former President John F. Kennedy—,was the insider here, and in spite of being a Kennedy, and having the endorsement of then powerful US House Speaker Nancy Pelosi, he still lost in another huge, even *massive* election upset. One headline of a local paper went like this: "Kennedy Loss in Massachusetts May Mark End of 'Camelot' Era."[44] Maybe. And perhaps it was also one more sign of this structural shift to the Left.

But this leftwards shift was not just changing *local* elections. *Nationally* Democrats were also benefiting from such far-left wins. Modcrate Joe Biden, for instance, carried the state of Georgia back in 2020 during his presidential run then, but largely thanks to the leftwing Black grassroots organizers that

---

[42] *https://www.msn.com/en-us/news/elections-2020/the-protests-are-already-changing-elections*
https://www.theatlantic.com/politics/archive/2020/06/jamaal-bowman-blm-booker-protests/613432/

[43] *https://www.wsj.com/us-news/socialists-zohran-mamdani-2008-financial-crisis-f98e54fa*

[44] *https://www.nbcboston.com/news/local/kennedy-loss-in-massachusetts-may-mark-end-of-camelot-era/2188785/*

had been rising there, and led then by a prominent progressive figure here, Stacy Abrams, a one-time state congresswoman. The importance of Abrams in this election could hardly be overstated, since she had led to a shift to the Left in a "longtime GOP [Republican] bastion of Georgia," as the Associated Press noted, and then adding, perhaps a bit too dramatically, also "—potentially remaking presidential politics for years to come."[45]

One more example of this "lefty insurgency" came from Buffalo, NY, where, in 2021, yet one more Democratic Socialist, India Walton, beat yet one more Democrat "insider," Buffalo's four-term mayor Byron Brown, a fixture of this city's politics for more than a decade. But India Walton beat him anyway, the first woman major of this city, the second-largest in the State of New York. During her campaign, Walton also stuck to issues dear to voters: affordable housing, health reform; and the reforming of the criminal justice system.[46] Prior to this, Walton had been a nurse and Union leader. And as a Black candidate, she could be seen as part of that newer trend among Black voters also shifting to the Left. Today, no less than 60% of Blacks thought of *socialism* with a "positive connotation," by far the highest such rate seen in any demographic group in the country.[47]

Socialism, of course, was nowhere close to getting any kind of a majority *nationally*. According to Gallup, only 47% of Americans said they would ever vote for a socialist president in 2019.[48]

---

[45] *https://apnews.com/article/election-2020-joe-biden-race-and-ethnicity-virus-outbreak-georgia-7a843bbce00713cfde6c3fdbc2e31eb7* Also see about Stacey Adams in: *https://www.bbc.com/news/world-us-canada-54875344*

[46] *https://apnews.com/article/buffalo-health-care-reform-government-and-politics-72e99937b2b11267c667b2b3d017606f*

[47] *https://www.axios.com/americas-continued-move-toward-socialism-84a0dda7-4b8d-483a-8c4e-0c2e562c4e67.html*

[48] *https://news.gallup.com/poll/254120/less-half-vote-socialist-president.aspx*
https://www.pewresearch.org/politics/2018/08/09/an-examination-of-the-2016-

And yet, the leftward shift here was still producing more electoral victories. In November 2021, in the city of Boston, for instance, voters again shifted Left, electing a progressive (not socialist) Democratic Mayor, Michelle Wu. She was an outsider, and a protégé of progressive Senator Elizabeth Warren. She then soon pushed for stemming the surging housing costs. She, for instance, wanted to limit annual rent increases to the consumer price index, plus 6%, but capping them at a 10% maximum. And this went beyond just Boston. In 2026, Wu also endorsed a potential, more restrictive, statewide rent control ballot initiative to a broader, state-wide strategy. In short, this progressive stance seemed try to spread, and go beyond just large metropolitan areas with lots of more progressive voters.

And yet one more example of this shift to the Left came from the 2023 progressive victory of a teacher's Union organizer, Brandon Johnson, this in the race for Mayor of Chicago, after he defeated then heavily favored Democrat insider Paul Vallas. Johnson also championed the working folk, speaking "regularly about 'investing in people,'" and had being funded largely by Unions, with his platform then including the idea of a class-based tax for the wealthiest, including "a higher real estate transfer tax on properties worth more than $1 million," as the *Chicago Tribune* reported back then.[49]

It's true that in spite of all these far-left wins, the far-right was still accelerating in it rise, especially after Trump's 2024 victory as US President. But it was also equally true that the far-left was also advancing, and, one might even argue, even accelerating its progress.

One example of this might be the victory of the charismatic

---

electorate-based-on-validated-voters/
https://www.chicagotribune.com/politics/elections/ct-chicago-mayor-election-winner-declared-20230405-plratgzcbrewbngbjcsxwmycgi-story.html

[49] *https://www.chicagotribune.com/politics/elections/ct-chicago-mayor-election-winner-declared-20230405-plratgzcbrewbngbjcsxwmycgi-story.html*

democratic socialist Zohan Mamdani, who unexpectedly beat the political super-heavyweight Mario Cuomo for Mayor of New York City, an amazing feat, accomplished, yet again, by grassroots campaigning, and by sticking to issues near and dear to voters, such as rent control, for instance.[50] Mamdani's triumph here right away sent shockwaves through the political landscape. President Trump immediately fired back: "He [Mamdani] is going to have problems with Washington like no Mayor in the history of our once great City," he wrote in TruthSocial. "Remember, he needs money from me, as President, in order to fulfill all of his FAKE Communist promises. He won't be getting any of it, so what's the point of voting for him?"[51] But Mamdani's win could still be a significant advancement in this new wave of democratic socialists. He has not yet moderated his radical stances for city-owned non-profit grocery stores; universal childcare; fare-free buses; and a rent freeze for about one million rent-stabilized units; and to do this all by taxing the wealthy and corporations with a flat 2% tax on incomes over $1 million, and also jacking up the corporate tax rate to 11.5%. Mamdani also wanted to keep his large grassroots volunteer base active by establishing a new and dedicated City Hall office to ensure its participation in all subsequent initiatives. If anything, the far-left here seemed to be turning increasingly bold, if only in certain urban corners, and only after that trying perhaps to spread this push towards their surrounding areas, as with Major Wu in Boston, who wanted to spread rent rise caps beyond this city.

The far-left was also pushing mainstream Democrats towards more radical stands. According to *The Wall Street*

---

[50] *https://www.wsj.com/politics/elections/nyc-mayor-democrat-zohran-mamdani-andrew-cuomo-1217fbfc*

[51] *https://www.nbcnewyork.com/new-york-city/trump-mamdani-comments-communist-adams-nyc-mayor-race/6397822/*

Journal, for instance, US Senate Minority Leader, Chuck Schumer, decided to cave in to the far-left pushes to fight Trump's severe 2025 cuts to healthcare. Schumer and mainstream Congress Democrats then went "all in" into a socialist-inspired fight, shutting down the US government, and displaying a much more radical leftwing type of challenge here, one that, in the end, although not successful, still led to the longest government shutdown in US history.[52]

Also in 2025, in the city of Seattle, a democratic socialist community organizer, Katie Wilson, won the mayoral election, and also by focusing on grassroots demands, especially the high cost of living, and the housing crisis. She also successfully framed herself as an outsider, fighting then the "status quo" incumbent Bruce Harrell, which she portrayed as a fixture of the establishment. Wilson then narrowly defeated Harrell by roughly 2,011 votes, the closest mayoral race in this city's modern history.

The taxing of the superrich was also taken up by Unions, progressives, and socialists in California. The proposed 2026 California Billionaire Tax Act, for instance, would impose a 5% tax on residents with over $1 billion in assets, and was primarily backed by the Service Employees International Union, and by United Healthcare Workers West (SEIU and UHW), and Senator Bernie Sanders, and various progressive, labor-aligned groups. The initiative also supported was by Congressman Ro Khanna, a self-described "progressive capitalist," reflecting a dual focus on social equity and the potential of American innovation.

The George Floyd protests

This structural shift to the Left might also be seen in the 2020

[52] *https://www.wsj.com/politics/policy/government-shutdown-democrats-trump-cadec6cd*

killing of a 46-year-old a Black man, George Floyd, while in custody by the Minneapolis PD. His murder here was recorded by a bystander, and then posted on the internet, and sparked the huge wave of protests, soon to rise under the banner of Black Lives Matter. They spread even to "small towns with deeply conservative politics," places with fewer than 20,000 residents. Usually led by "small numbers of black students with lots of teenage allies, plus some older supporters," the protests were so strong they seemed like a throwback to the 1950s and 1960s, but different in that they came not only from cities and college campuses, but also from small, white, conservative towns in Idaho, like Coeur d'Alene, say, places where just two decades earlier the Aryan Nations supremacists had been marching.[53] *The Wall Street Journal* also noticed here, "just how widespread and fast-moving the movement is."[54] It also led to a "huge surge" in voter registrations among Democrats. Most here were young, and *women*, which, according to polls, favored more liberal causes, including, at times, even socialism —with almost half of US women (45%) reporting now having "positive connotations" towards socialism.[55] Online donations here also grew by a surprising 70%, just in 2020.[56] Other polls also showed the public being "more troubled" by the killing of George Floyd than by the sporadic violence and looting. Finally, among *average* Americans, there was now an incredible 2-to-1 margin support *in favor* of the protesters, according to one poll

---

[53] *https://www.washingtonpost.com/politics/2020/06/06/floyd-protests-are-broadest-us-history-are-spreading-white-small-town-america/*

[54] *https://www.wsj.com/articles/black-lives-matter-protests-spread-quickly-to-white-rural-areas-11592818201*

[55] *https://www.axios.com/americas-continued-move-toward-socialism-84a0dda7-4b8d-483a-8c4e-0c2e562c4e67.html*

[56] Breakdown of voters registered with Rock the Vote: 70% under 30 years of age; 76% women; 39% self-defined as people of color; 42% of under-30s were people of color. *https://www.cnbc.com/2020/06/05/george-floyd-protests-created-surge-in-voter-registrations-groups-say.html*

in *The Wall Street Journal*.[57]

Black Lives Matters also spelled disaster for President Donald Trump's bid for reelection in 2020, and perhaps being a significant factor that stopped him from gaining a second consecutive term in this office.[58] The examples here seem rather convincing. Even a traditionally Republican state like Michigan, that year flipped to the Democrats, and largely thanks to the Black Lives Matters protests, which, in Michigan, were backed by organizations such as Detroit Action, Michigan Liberation, We The People, and People's Action. *The Wall Street Journal* pointed out again how the George Floyd protests had the effect of "reshaping the 2020 campaign."[59] Exit polls even showed protests having at least "a role" among most voters' decisions, with a fifth of voters here believing that these "protests were [actually] the single most important factor at the ballot box."[60]

Women

Between 1994 and 2018, American women went from being core Republican voters, to core Democrat ones —a more than 30 percentage point shift towards the Left in 22 years, according to the *Wall Street Journal*.[61] This was historic. No wonder Hillary Clinton then gained so much more traction in

---

[57] *https://www.wsj.com/articles/americans-are-more-troubled-by-police-actions-in-killing-of-george-floyd-than-by-violence-at-protests-poll-finds-11591534801*

[58] See for instance: *https://www.niskanencenter.org/how-protests-change-parties-and-elections/*

[59] *https://www.wsj.com/graphics/two-michigan-counties-show-protests-reshaping-2020-campaign/https://www.nytimes.com/2020/11/07/us/black-lives-matter-protests.html*

[60] *https://www.nytimes.com/2020/11/07/us/black-lives-matter-protests.html*

[61] The polls said that 43% of women felt the need to protest, against only 28% among men. Interestingly, men without bachelor's degrees here had moved further to the Right, a shift that had actually accelerated after 2008, which helped explain the support for Donald Trump. *https://www.wsj.com/articles/the-yawning-divide-that-explains-american-politics-1540910719*

2016; and also that the 2017 Women's March became the largest single-day protest in all of US history, at least according to one study.[62]

American women were spearheading here a structural shift to the Left, and with unexpected results. The medical profession, for instance, had been traditionally a core Republican stronghold for at least half a century, and a huge source for rightwing donations. But the rising numbers of women in the field now entering the American Medical Association —the main medical association in the country— was shifting this once rightwing organization towards more liberal ideals, including universal healthcare, something almost unthinkable just a few decades earlier.[63]

Finally, the rising radicalism among women seemed to be visible in that women were now (in 2018) almost twice as likely to feel the need to protest as men, and with the top issues for women here being women's rights, followed by immigration rights and gun control.[64]

Universal Income

Americans were at their most conservative around *economic* ideologies, or policies. Usually, less than one in five US voters supported the liberals around the economy, their lowest support in any policy area. But even here, support in recent times for liberal economic ideologies has gone up from 17% to 21% between 2002 and 2020, according to *The Economist.*[65]

---

[62] *https://www.independent.co.uk/news/world/americas/womens-march-anti-donald-trump-womens-rights-largest-protest-demonstration-us-history-political-a7541081.html*

[63] *https://www.wsj.com/articles/doctors-once-gop-stalwarts-now-more-likely-to-be-democrats-11570383523*

[64] *https://news.gallup.com/poll/241634/one-three-americans-felt-urge-protest.aspx*

[65] *https://news.gallup.com/poll/311303/americans-remain-liberal-socially-economically.aspx*

This was first fueled by the Basic Universal Income, or UBI —or free money for everyone— debate during the 2020 Covid-19 pandemic, and after large swaths of the economy here simply shut down at this time.[66] Just between February and April of that same year, support for UBI in the US rose from 43% to 49%. And support for *emergency* payments, plus an extra year of free money, gained an incredible *majority* among all Americans at that time, reaching a record high never before seen in the country of 66%. Even a majority of *Republicans* (52%) supported UBI at this time, with UBI here then becoming so popular that it even became a *bipartisan* issue. This support, of course, didn't last forever, but it was still an example of how quickly public opinion can shift to the Left in this respect, even around the economy, if times become severe enough in a crisis.[67]

Libertarians, of course, hated UBI. They said it promoted social "infantalization," dependency; the killing of America's entrepreneurial spirit. But, again, the biggest supporters of UBI in the US were the young, which backed it by a whopping 72% in 2020.[68] The youth, after all, was the one faced the highest rates of debt and unemployment of any generation, and were then the most likely to shift to the Left in this area, showing again how quickly this leftward shift could *accelerate* in the US

---

[66] See, for instance, the article on Sanders' goal to provide basic necessities for all. *https://news.gallup.com/opinion/polling-matters/285839/sanders-goal-provide-basic-necessities.aspx*

[67] *https://thehill.com/hilltv/rising/463055-more-voters-support-universal-basic-income.*
https://news.gallup.com/poll/267143/universal-basic-income-favored-canada-not.aspx
Also: https://theappeal.org/majority-of-americans-support-monthly-cash-assistance-to-offset-pandemic-damage-to-economy/

[68] Youth here includes those aged 18 to 34. Interestingly, Andrew Yang was the Democrat that supported UI in 2019, not Bernie Sanders, who argued that "people want to work." See: *https://thehill.com/hilltv/rising/463055-more-voters-support-universal-basic-income*

as soon as the economy seems to be falling apart in any significant way, as might happen, for instance, in a recession or, more so, in a depression.

But why then hasn't a major shift to the Left happened already? If the Left was already gaining so much *structural* ground, why hasn't politics already shifted Left? The main reason might be that voters were still in a strong anti-government mood, the dominant once since the mid-1970s, and the longest in history, and, thus, very deeply ingrained.[69] Deep anti-government moods make it harder for the Left to expand, since the Left needs the government action to regulate the economy, and redistribute income. But if people distrust the government so much, how can the Left then rise and go for government-led regulations and redistribution policies?

---

[69] Voters still remained very anti-government, with one poll finding that most in 2015 still stood against a more "government-managed economy," at 66%. Less than a third supported a more "government-managed economy."
http://reason.com/blog/2015/02/12/poll-americans-like-free-markets-more-t2

2. DEPRESSIONS AND BIG SHIFTS TO THE LEFT

In the US, all *major* shifts to the Left have come from economic depressions. This has been a pattern seen for at least the last 200 years. This happened during the Depression of 1837, for instance, America's first great depression. It began, as with all others, with a financial panic. In New Orleans the price of cotton, back then a top US export, suddenly crashed, falling by half. New York banks, caught in this panic, then also suddenly refused to redeem paper money for gold or silver, leaving many customers with worthless currency. Out of 850 American banks, around 343 closed for good at this time. Southern cotton planters, particularly in Mississippi, were ruined, with many abandoning plantations, and fleeing to Texas to avoid debtors' prison. One British diplomat traveling through New Orleans at this time reported the country presenting "a lamentable appearance of exhaustion and demoralization."[70] Railroad construction was also stopped; factories shut down

[70] *https://www.americanyawp.com/text/09-democracy-in-america/*

due to this dried-up credit; and the publishing industry was severely impacted. Unable to pay back loans, eight US states defaulted on their loans during this time, destroying their credit. Unemployment shot up to about 25% in some parts, causing families to lose their homes and to struggle now to afford basic necessities like food and clothing —typical signs of a depression. Two-thirds of New Yorkers now were with "no means of support," and hunger became so widespread that, in some parts, authorities had to hand out emergency food. Despair sparked riots and intense unrest. As one newspaper reported: "there has never been a time like this," with "rumor after rumor of riot, insurrection, and tumult."[71] The 1837 Depression lasted for almost a decade, leading voters to turn against then President Martin Van Buren, a fiscally conservative, rightwing, and spend-cutting president, who had formerly been quite popular, but that now, with the economy crashing, had turned unpopular. The public now turn away from its prior anti-government mood, and, in a major shift to the Left, now gave its full support to road-building, job-creating, "economic nationalist" policies championed by the new liberal Whig Party leader of this time, William Henry Harrison.[72] These were, of course, typical policies of the Left: more government intervention and regulation to help those in need; and to try to stimulate the economy. Harrison won the 1840 presidential race by a landslide —wining 42.4% of the popular vote, and 234 of the total 294 electoral votes, and completely reversing the balance of power in American politics for decades.[73] It was, in short, a massive shift to the Left, with the more liberal Whig Party then going on to win two more

---

[71] Quoted in: Fraser, Caroline. *Prairie Fires. The American Dreams of Laura Ingalls Wilder.* New York, NY: Metropolitan Books, 2017, p. 33-34.

[72] *https://www.history.com/topics/us-presidents/martin-van-buren*

[73] *https://www.presidency.ucsb.edu/statistics/data/voter-turnout-in-presidential-elections*

presidential elections after that, also by large margins. And it was the depression that fueled this *major* shift to the Left, and towards public spending, and more nationalist and anti-immigrant policy. After being hit by terrible economic times, Americans now clamored for regulations; for protectionism; for more government oversight; and for more officially-funded projects to give people jobs, and all *within* a democratic system. In short, it was a major shift to the Left, the first since America's independence.

This was the time when far-left authors became so popular, as, for instance, with Henry David Thoreau, now openly attacking the rich and promoting anarchist-sounding ideals such as, "The rich man is always sold to the institution which makes him rich," or government, fostering, thus, an alliance of corrupt business elites with corrupt government elites to help secure overwhelming wealth and power for such elites.

This was the time also of the rise of the Liberty Party, an abolitionist party formed in 1840 which declared its aim "the absolute and unqualified divorce of the general government from slavery, and also the restoration of equality of rights among men, in every State where the party exists, or may exist," a radical stance for this time, foreshadowing America's later Civil War abolitionism.[74] In 1848, this Liberty Party also led to the rise of another egalitarian party, the Free Soil Party, dedicated to opposing the expansion of slavery into newly acquired western US territory, and of championing egalitarian principles.

This *major* shift to the Left only lost steam until the 1850s, but only *after* the US economy began to recover, and rise again into growth during these years. The anti-government mood among the public came back, and under such sentiments the

[74] McKee, Thomas Hudson. *The National Conventions and Platforms of All Political Parties 1789-1905*. Sydney, New South Wales: Wentworth Press, 2016, p. 52.

Left did ever more poorly here.

This has been how all such big shifts to the Left work. They only last while depressions last. Once the hard times are over, the country again shifts back to the Right.[75] As the old Wall Street saying goes: "socialism on way down; capitalism on the way up." This happened also during the 1850s, as the economy improved, with public mood shifting rightwards, eventually leaving behind the Whig Party, and then going back to the old "free market," *laissez faire*, and free enterprise policies of the Right, with all its basic and boilerplate ideals, and fueling the rise of the then more rightwing Republican Party, and causing the collapse of the Whig Party during the mid-1850s, which then officially dissolved in 1860.

"Socialism on way down; capitalism on the way up."

The next *big* shift to the Left then only happened until 1873, and again it only came to be because America was once more hit by a depression, today known as the *Long Depression*. This long depression was triggered by a Panic in 1873, the result of a "perfect storm" of railroad overexpansion, risky banking practices, and global monetary shifts. It caused the bankruptcy of the nation's then premier investment bank, Jay Cooke & Company, which had overextended itself by financing the Northern Pacific Railway. The bank was then forced to close, sparking a massive loss of public confidence, leading to a "domino effect" of bank runs throughout the country. It also led to the first-ever 10-day closure of the New York Stock Exchange. This collapse led to a billion dollars of private debt going unpaid, a just massive sum of money for this time. Cotton prices crashed, as did the agricultural economy in general, and

---

[75] A paper by two British political scientists also saw this same pattern, but at a smaller scale, with Britain's leftwing Labour Party shifting Right when the economy was okay, but moving Left when the economy seemed to be in trouble. *https://journals.sagepub.com/doi/full/10.1177/13691481221099734*

particularly in the South. Thousands of businesses failed. Hundreds of thousands of workers lost their jobs. A quarter of workers in New York City, for instance, ended on the streets, and facing such dire economic times, yet again, public mood shifted to the Left, and away from the typical rightwing "free market" ideals from the 1850s and 60s. Public mood shifted towards pro-government policies, and politics to the Left, towards more government intervention, regulation, and economic stimulus. The main beneficiary was the Democratic Party, the more liberal one at this time, and just one year into this Long Depression, this party reversed decades of losses by the Left, and in 1874 went to win a massive majority in the House of Representatives, a first for this party since the Civil War, and a major reversal for American politics. This giant flip was perhaps the biggest such flip in favor of the Left in the House in all of US history, with Democrats here winning a stunning 94 extra seats, and completely reversing the balance of power from this era.[76] As was usual, the Left here did well only under a pro-government regulation sentiment, which, with the Long Depression, was on the rise now in the country.

America also saw the rise of its first socialist party now, the Socialist Labor Party, founded in 1876. The country also of its first broad, *nationwide* worker strike, the Great Railway Strike of 1877, mobilizing some 100,000 workers across the country, a first in US history.[77] The unrest here was simply massive. In Pittsburg alone, strikers destroyed 39 buildings, 104 locomotives, and 1,245 train cars.[78] Although short-lived, the strike for the first time gave US labor a permanent place in the country's politics, and a newfound "electoral appeal," and an

---

[76] *https://history.house.gov/Institution/Majority-Changes/Majority-Changes/*

[77] *https://www.britannica.com/topic/Great-Railroad-Strike-of-1877*

[78] Stoller, Matt. *Goliath: The 100-Year War Between Monopoly Power and Democracy.* New York, NY: Simon & Schuster, 2019, p. 8.

unprecedented "legitimacy in respectable discourse," as one specialist historian from this era, Richard Schneirov, once put it.[79]

American workers also created now the country's first nationwide labor organization: the American Federation of Labor, founded 1886, and still in existence today.

Also at this time, in 1888, American voters elected the first left-leaning president in decades, Benjamin Harrison, who had run at this time on protectionism and tariffs policies to stimulate the economy, create jobs, and rejecting rightwing "free trade" policies. And just two years after that, in 1890, a Democrat-controlled US Congress passed the Sherman Antitrust Act, aimed at busting monopolies, another major first for the country, and clearly a leftwing undertaking. And just two years after that, in 1892, there was yet one more huge strike, the Homestead Strike against the giant Carnegie Steel Company, perhaps the country's quintessential example struggle against its business elites, or, as they were called back then, the Robber Barons.

The progressive push here went well beyond just labor. The Sierra Club was founded also in 1892, formed in San Francisco by the naturalist John Muir and a group of California intellectuals, and all part of this same progressive movement. This organization still exists today as a core liberal group, again showing the durability of leftwing or progressive organizations in the US since this time.

The Long Depression was a "double-dip" depression, made of *two* successive major economic downturns: one *first* hitting the country in 1873; and a *second* dip hitting it in 1893. But either dip could be seen as a depression. During the first dip,

---

[79] Schneirov, Richard. *Labor and Urban Politics: Class Conflict and the Origins of Modern Liberalism in Chicago, 1864–97*. Urbana, IL: University of Illinois Press, 1998, p. 4.

five hundred of the country's banks permanently closed their doors, and about 15,000 businesses failed nationwide. Unemployment shot up to horrific levels, in Pennsylvania reaching 25%; and in New York 35%; and in Michigan 43%. Many faced starvation, much like back in 1837, with charities yet again opening their doors with soup kitchens for the hungry —just as it would happen also later, during the 1930s Great Depression. Voters during the Long Depression again cried out for government assistance, while "free markets" and *laissez faire* policies went out of favor, and were even scorned and reviled by much of the public back then. The public mood of the nation had *completely* reversed itself, and Americans moved again to the Left, and in a big way, *again*.

This major shift to the Left also led, in 1891, to the rise of America's first "populist" party, the People's Party —one in favor of the common person, and against the privileged elites that ignored them. The People's Party called for "significant social change," and believed in "using public authority to redistribute private wealth and to regulate the banks and industrial corporation that... dominated the American economy." Notice the typical pro-government leftwing rhetoric here: *more* regulation; *more* egalitarianism; *more* grassroots control over the country. The People's Party pioneered the vote for women, too, another central egalitarian principle, and even called for the nationalization of all US railroads, the radical opposite of the "free market" approach of past rightwing governments. Its master orator, William Jennings Bryan, or the "Great Commoner," as he was then called, gave this People's Party its clear, powerful voice, with Bryan's commanding lines here becoming hugely famous, including his celebrated one about not crucifying "men to a cross of gold" —and thus defending silver as the common person's currency, or "poor man's gold." Bryan might have failed to make large inroads among many city voters, including the urban middle classes, but his radical speeches and core Christian beliefs widely appealed to farmers, which at this time were still a very large part of the total national vote, and who flocked in droves to support him.[80]

The second dip of the Long Depression hit the US in 1893 with another massive financial crisis that unleashed the worst depression in the nation's history up to that point. Over 15,000 businesses and 500 to 600 banks failed in 1893 alone. Approximately one-fourth of all U.S. railroad mileage went into receivership. At its peak, national unemployment soared now to between 17% and 20%, and in some industrial states like New York and Michigan, rates here reached as high as 35% to 43%.[81]

With no federal social safety net, millions faced starvation and homelessness. This led to the creation of soup kitchens and local relief efforts like Detroit's Potato Patch Plan during the mid-1890s of community gardens to feed the hungry.[82]

The crisis also sparked violent strikes, most notably the Pullman Strike of 1894, where federal troops had to be sent in to restore rail traffic.

A group of workers in 1895 in Ohio launched a march of thousands of unemployed onto the capital Washington, DC, called the *Army of the Commonwealth in Christ*, gaining some 20,000 followers, and becoming the first such march on Washington DC. Also known as the Industrial Army, or Coxey's Army, after its main organizer, it demanded the government *directly* hire workers to build infrastructure, and give them work at public expense —an idea that would only become a

---

[80] Foner, Eric. "Hope in the Desert," in *London Review of Books*. May 12, 2022, p. 13.

[81] *https://www.federalreservehistory.org/essays/banking-panics-of-the-gilded-age*

[82] Parshall, Gerald. "The Great Panic Of '93" in *U.S. News & World Report*, 113.17 (1992).

reality three decades later, under the 1930s New Deal by FDR, and the next economic depression to hit the nation.

Again, this 1893 depression shifted public mood in favor of the government, and this pro-government sentiment fueled the rise of major leftwing shifts in US policies.

Some economic recovery did begin in around 1897, aided by a surge in gold discoveries (such as the Klondike Gold Rush), and a rise in international demand for American agricultural products following some crop failures in Europe. Still, shaken by that double-dip Long Depression in 1873, and then again in 1893, America continued to feel a weariness towards "free markets," and kept an overall Left-bound shift by forming a second socialist party in the country in 1901, the Socialist Party of America; and just four years after that, in 1905, the country's first socialist labor organization, the Industrial Workers of the World, or "Wobblies," again, part of this huge leftwards shift fueled by the long sufferings caused by the double-dip Long Depression, and keeping this leftwards shift going until well into the early 1900s.

And in case Americans had forgotten then the dangers of financial crises, in 1907 the country was hit yet again by another panic, and again the finances of Wall Street crashed, and workers and middle classes again suffered. This then "sped up the process of reform," as American labor historian Howard Zinn once explained, leading to a "growing strength of the Socialists, Wobblies, and trade unions,"[83] and to a further push Left in American politics, even at this very late time.

The trauma of the 1893 depression dip fed a major leftwards shift known then as the Progressive Era, even into the early 20th century, starting with the "Bull Moose" Party in 1912, founded by former President Theodore Roosevelt, after

---

[83] Zinn, Howard. *A People's History of the United States.* New York: HarperCollins, 1980, p. 342.

he lost the Republican nomination to then incumbent President William Howard Taft. Roosevelt here was frustrated by the conservative turn the Republican Party had taken at this time. It was then that Roosevelt and his progressive supporters walked out of this party's convention, forming their own party to champion more leftwing, pro-government regulation and egalitarian ideals, including women's suffrage, labor laws, and corporate regulation. With more support among city folk and middle classes, these progressives pushed against the super-rich, and against their excessive fortunes, against the Robber Barons, their monopolies, and their pervasive corruption. Roosevelt here even called these super-rich the "malefactors of great wealth," and "the predator man of wealth."[84] Three of the most notable presidents of this era were all progressives: Teddy Roosevelt, William Howard Taft, and Woodrow Wilson. And as the historian Daniel Sjursen once pointed out, even the more rightwing of them, Wilson, wasn't too far behind in his progressivism. "Wilson's first term seemed a Progressive dream," Sjursen noted here, with President Wilson having then "abolished child labor, and passing a new antitrust act, and an eight-hour work week, and federal aid to farmers."[85] In truth child labor was outright banned only two decades later, with the 1930s New Deal, but such reforms were, nonetheless, still fairly radical for their time.

The tail end of this vast shift to the Left in the US only came to an end at during the early decades of the 21st century, with the triumph of the suffragette movement, which finally gave women the vote in 1920, a last major victory for leftwing egalitarian values. Also in 1920, came Prohibition, banning the

---

[84] Quoted in: Nations, Scott. *A History of the United States in Five Crashes*. New York, NY: William Morrow, 2017, pp. 23-24.

[85] Sjursen, Daniel A. *A True History of the United States*. Lebannon, NH: Steerforth Press, 2021, p. 262.

manufacture, sale, and transportation of alcoholic beverages,[86] perhaps one of the most radical government interventions in the economy ever in the US, and a clear departure from rightwing "free markets" and "free enterprise." The progressive era had been, thus, decidedly egalitarian, anti-oligarchic, and pro-government regulation, the opposite of most rightwing, "free market" values.

The Long Depression left a deep mark on American politics. It fueled powerful nationwide strikes, Unions, nationwide workers associations, and the pro-farmer and pro-worker People's Party, and the remarkably influential Progressive Era, and the rise of two socialist parties, and one socialist worker organization, all first time events in US history. The Long Depression only ran out of steam until 1917, with the entrance of the US into World War I in Europe. And as the US economy again recovered, shaking off the dark shadow of the Long Depression, it led then to the prosperous 1920s, or Roaring 20s, when US markets again grew rapidly, the public turned yet again anti-government, and seduced yet again by those old promises of prosperity under the pro-business slogans of "free markets," and "free enterprise."

During the 1920s, the US economy experienced indeed a very rapid growth, with its GNP rising by over 40%, fueled by mass production, still mostly a novelty back then, and by technological innovation, and high consumer demand. Following a relatively tame 1920-1921 recession, America's economic boom here featured a 4.2% annual growth, and a thriving stock market, and increased suburban development, and even though some agricultural sectors struggled, and wealth inequality rose during this decade,[87] the Robber Barons

---

[86] *http://projects.vassar.edu/1896/depression.html*

[87] *https://rainford.org.uk/wp-content/uploads/2021/05/9.9-The-economic-boom-in-the-1920s.pdf*

and oligarchs of the Progressive Era, now again became salient industrialists and "captains of industry," championing the same narrative of technological advances, holding the great promises of future affluence and fortune for all under a "free market" system.

The *Wall Street Journal* of that time —the *Magazine of Wall Street*— even proudly proclaimed: "As Rome had its Agustinian Age and Britain had its Victorian Age, so are we to enter an epoch of affluence and magnificence."[88] A famous 1920s Yale economics professor, Irving Fisher, argued the US was poised now to grow for many decades, all due to the extraordinary rise of new technologies such as the radio and the automobile. Optimism was back; the Left was out; and the future now belonged to "free markets," to "free enterprise," and, of course, to the Right.

Under such prosperous times, full of *affluence and magnificence*, people didn't need government help anymore, and left-leaning Democrats now faced "staggering losses" at the polls during the 1920s. Anti-government sentiment was back on the rise, and more government regulation no longer appealed as much to the voters. Democrats then faced an almost catastrophic 1924 convention, with attendees here falling into such disarray that they required more than a hundred rounds of voting just to agree on the nomination of that year's presidential candidate. The comedian Will Rodgers even joked back then: "I'm not a member of an organized political party. I'm a Democrat."[89]

Now the right-leaning Republican Party made a major comeback, as a pro-business, isolationist party. For most of the 1920s, Republicans also went go on to control both the

---

[88] Quoted in: Morgan, Ted. *A Covert Life: Jay Lovestone: Communist, Anti-Communist, Spymaster*. New York, NY; Random House, 1999, p. 78.

[89] Foner, Eric. "Hope in the Desert," in *London Review of Books*. May 12, 2022, p. 13.

presidency, and both houses of Congress, the House and the Senate. Republican Presidents like Warren Harding now called for a "return to normalcy" after the reform-minded Progressive Era. Republican President Calvin Coolidge, and President Herbert Hoover were now champions again of *laissez-faire*, and "free markets," and for lower taxes, high tariffs, and minimal government intervention in the economy. The postwar boom seemed to call for stability more than for change, with the Republican Party now encouraging non-social values such as that of "rugged individualism," and "free enterprise" as the key to success and industrial growth. President Coolidge, in office between 1923 and 1929, even said that "the chief business of the American people is business."

Of course, the Roaring 20s, its nearly endless faith in *affluence and magnificence*, and its corresponding shift to the Right did not last forever. This 1920s expansion only lasted for about 20 years, if counting from the mid-1910s until 1929. At this point, the economy crashed again, and this time even worse than during the mid-1870s and 90s. This time, the stock market fell in value by nearly 80% *in just one year*. Markets in general shrunk by an incredible 90%, and the economy fell by 36% if measured by its GDP, all absolutely a stunning drops, and from which the US would not fully recover until *25 years later*.[90] Unemployment shot up to 25% —and much higher in larger cities, where it likely reached 30%, or more. About 9,000 banks closed nationwide, and, collectively, they lost some $140 billion dollars in private deposits, an absolutely cataclysmic sum of money for this time; decimating life savings, workers, farmers, and middle classes. Consumer prices fell by *two thirds*, leading into outright *deflation*. The price of chicken, for instance, fell from 38 cents a pound to just 12; the price of eggs

---

[90] *https://www.investopedia.com/ask/answers/042115/what-caused-stock-market-crash-1929-preceded-great-depression.asp*

fell from 50 cents a dozen to just over 13 cents; and yet many in America could still not afford to buy them, even at these much lower prices.[91] It was what economists would now call "demand destruction."

The 1930s *Great Depression* had begun, and just like all prior depressions, it led to another huge shift to the Left among voters.

The last of the 1920s rightwing Republican presidents, Herbert Hoover, elected in 1928, continued with the anti-government ideals of "free markets" well into the 1930s, insisting that the depression was a temporary setback, and still calling for people to have patience, assuring them that recovery was "just around the corner."

But this time Americans didn't go for it, and cried now for help again, and yet again turned to pro-government stances, including government aid. Gone were all the 1920s anti-government sentiments. Americans again voted Democrats back into office, and in a *massive* way again, leaving the "free market" Republicans in the dust. Just one year into this depression, in 1930, and in a single swoop, voters flipped the US House of Representatives fully in favor of the Democrats, giving them 52 extra seats.[92] And just two years after that, in 1932, Democrats won the presidency, electing Franklin Delano Roosevelt's by a huge margin; winning 472 electoral votes against just 59 for the then incumbent Herbert Hoover, one of the most crushing defeats in US election history. After that, Roosevelt went on to win *four* successive presidencies, the most successful president ever, if measured by this scale at least,[93] and a sign perhaps of how deeply scared the Great

---

[91] *https://www.stlouisfed.org/~/media/files/pdfs/great-depression/the-great-depression-wheelock-overview.pdf*

[92] *https://history.house.gov/Institution/Majority-Changes/Majority-Changes/*

[93] *https://www.britannica.com/event/United-States-presidential-election-of-1932*

Depression had left the American public, even after two decades after the 1929 crash.

Clearly, the country had shifted to the Left in a *big* way again. And this was only due to having fallen into a depression. Roosevelt at this time changed America. He launched the Emergency Banking Act and the Federal Deposit Insurance Corporation, or FDIC, to protect depositors from bank runs. He created the Farm Security Administration, aiming to resettle farmers, furnishing them with credit and technology. He created the Civilian Conservation Corps and the Civil Works Administration, both programs that, as Coxey's Army had asked for back in the 1890s (and never gotten), gave *direct* employment to workers in infrastructure projects. Roosevelt also abolished child labor for all kids under the age of 14, finally putting a full stop to this kind of labor abuse.[94] He also created the nation's first publicly funded unemployment insurance; the first publicly funded benefit funds for victims of industrial accidents; the first pensions for retired workers; and the first federal public aid for dependent mothers and children. He instituted government assistance for the blind and the handicapped. He set a minimum wage, a first also in US history, and been previously seen as an intolerable hindrance on "free markets." These changes brought real changes in the economy, and in just three years, the nation saw a drop in its economic inequality of about 30% —if measured by the share of the top earners as a part of the total national income.[95] It was the kind of egalitarian reform that the Left usually was pushing for, and done via government regulation, and even direct intervention

---

[94] *https://www.bls.gov/opub/mlr/2017/article/history-of-child-labor-in-the-united-states-part-1.htm*
https://www.bls.gov/opub/mlr/2017/article/history-of-child-labor-in-the-united-states-part-2-the-reform-movement.htm

[95] Tepper, Johnathan, and Denise Hearn. *The Myth of Capitalism: Monopolies and the Death of Competition.* Hoboken, NJ: John Wiley & Sons, 2019, p. 32.

in the economy.

The American elites were, of course, furious, and tried to overthrow Roosevelt. Secretly they organized a forceful plan to depose him, and put in power a rightwing authoritarian. Known as the White House Putsch, it involved ultra-rich American families and business leaders directly recruiting a veterans' organization led then by a retired Marine Corps General, Smedley Butler, seeking him to set up as the country's dictator. They failed, in large part because Butler himself, a man of exceptional honor and courage, it seems, denounced the plotters to the US Congress, foiling thus their attempt, and exposing most of the details of their secret plans to the public. The putsch mimic similar ones tried in Europe at this time, by fascists in Italy, and by Adolf Hitler in Germany. This event has been minimized and even ignored by later American history. But the effort was no small potatoes. A 1934 congressional report had concluded that, "there is no question that these attempts [at a business putsch] were discussed, were planned, and might have been placed in execution when and if the financial backers deemed it expedient."[96]

Branded a radical, even a socialist, Roosevelt's New Deal then pushed for protecting workers and farmers, and the middle classes. It might have seem radical to many, but the reforms here were actually a rather moderate, and happened only because Roosevelt was under massive pressure from many grassroots movements, insurgent voters, and regional leaders, forcing him to keep moving to the Left, even when he was not always fully convinced of these policies himself. The country had become a hotbed of grassroots radicalism. *Alabama* at this point had Black workers and sharecroppers organize a *communist* organization. There were also two huge

---

[96] *https://www.washingtonpost.com/history/2021/01/13/fdr-roosevelt-coup-business-plot/*

populist figures rising at this time: Louisiana's Senator Huey Long; and Detroit's radio personality, and Canadian-American Catholic priest, Charles Coughlin. Both have been forgotten, but back then they were Roosevelt's most radical challengers. Huey Long was the most successful of the two, wanting even to set up a wealth cap of one million dollars over all the rich, one of the most radical anti-elite initiatives ever attempted perhaps by a national figure in the US. This idea was also *incredibly popular amongst the public*, receiving huge backing for Long. So much so, it forced Roosevelt in 1935 to shift even further to the Left, starting what was later known as his Second New Deal, by raising income and inheritance taxes, including to the wealthiest. One Democrat senator at this time put it like this: "We are obliged to propose and accept many things in the New Deal that otherwise we would not because we must prevent a union of discontent around [Huey Long]. The President is the only hope of the conservatives and liberals; if his program is restricted, the answer may be Huey Long."[97]

Father Coughlin was also a radical. He called for an all-out *nationalizing* of all US "banking, credit and currency," and of all "power, light, oil and natural gas" companies, since they were, he proclaimed, "our God-given natural resources." He also proposed to get rid of the Federal Reserve, which he deemed, "the harsh, cruel and grasping ways of wicked men who first concentrated wealth in the hands of a few."[98] Again, these were among the most radical anti-elite efforts ever attempted by a nationwide political figure in US history.

Alarmed, Roosevelt's then interior secretary, Harold Ickes, put it like this: "The country is much more radical than the Administration." And Roosevelt, he said, "would have to move

---

[97] Quoted in: Brinkley, Alan. *Voices of Protests. Huey Long, Father Coughlin, & The Great Depression*. New York, NY: Vintage Books, 1983, p. 80.
[98] *Idem*, p. 287.

further to the left in order to hold the country." Roosevelt saw as his job to "save our system;" to save "the capitalist system from 'crackpot ideas'," as he himself put it. And by *crackpots*, he was almost certainly referring to Huey and Coughlin, and many other grassroots movements spreading around the country. Roosevelt's reforms were thus "designed to cut the ground from under the demagogues," as his son Elliot once explained. Their purpose: undermine populists, progressives, and socialists. The New Deal, in its ideology, was not progressive or populist, but really "as old as Christian ethics," as Roosevelt also put it. It was egalitarian; but it saw government regulation as a *moral* issue, not needing then any populist, socialist, or progressive ideals. And in keeping with this moral tone, Roosevelt once wrote: the New Deal "recognizes that man is indeed his brother's keeper... It demands that justice shall rule the mighty as well as the weak." And when he was once asked about his "philosophy," he replied: "Philosophy? Philosophy? I am a Christian and a Democrat —that's all."[99]

In saving "capitalism," Roosevelt was extremely successful. As one New Deal supporter realized: "Your administration [Roosevelt's administration] has made possible the continuance of American institutions for at least fifty years. You have done for the government what St. Francis did for the Catholic Church. You have brought it back to the people."[100]

Roosevelt had shifted to the Left in a major way, yes, but not by an inch more than was absolutely necessary. And he did so, only so that the ideas of Long and Coughlin could never make it into Law, and to avoid the many radical forces around the country to gather together into a nationwide, unified force to rival that of the Democratic Party. Roosevelt's jellyfish policies

---

[99] Quoted in: Sjursen, Daniel, *op cit.*, pp. 331 and 328.

[100] Quoted in: Talbot, David. *The Devil's Chessboard. Allen Dulles, the CIA, and the Rise of America's Secret Government.* New York, NY: HarperCollins, 2019, p. 63.

thus managed to absorb enough of push of these local and regional groups to blunt their ultimate force at nationally. And in time, such radicals faded. Huey was killed. And Father Coughlin after 1938 turned towards desperate attempts to stay relevant, such as embracing anti-Semitism. In the end, Roosevelt saved the elites, and kept their extraordinary power and influence more or less intact. Roosevelt did what all elites do when faced with radical times: they play the long game; yield as much as circumstances demand, and, over time, exhaust the radicals, and then keep their influence and privilege, reviving them at a later time. The elites know it: they are, in a way, eternal in this way.

But what really saved the economy was the outbreak of World War II. This meant the huge mobilization of vast armies and of vast sums of money and equipment to defeat Germans, Italians, and Japanese. It got America's industrial and agricultural might going on again. The mass spending brought the economy back to life. And after this war was over, the US was left with a giant global empire that opened the door for even more profits for American elites, thus propelling the nation into a new era of *unprecedented* prosperity; the exact opposite of the floundering economy of the 1930s.

This new postwar era would later be dubbed the "Golden Era of Capitalism." It was a new period that spanned a 32 year-long expansion of the economy, all the way from the mid-1940s until the early 1970s, and reaching well into the Richard Nixon administration. This massive expansion only ended with the 1973 Oil Shock. It amassed an impressive 169% overall expansion of the US economy; and an overall 75% rise in its employment; and it almost doubling the country's average personal income. It also pushed manufacturing up by 30%, and made "capitalism" work for more people than ever before. Well-regulated, dynamic, progressive, and even benefited the working classes, not just the few elites at the top.[101] "People of all incomes and education levels could [now] live the American Dream," as one author wrote, "and children were almost guaranteed to be better off than [their parents]."[102] Politics shifted Right again, starting with the 1947 Taft–Hartley Act busting Union power; and then continuing with the 1953-54 Red Scare, and Senator Joseph McCarthy's Anti-American Activities Committee, stamping out, as he said, all communists out of the US government. There was the Eisenhower Era, a moderate balance between liberal Democrats and conservative Republicans, so stable and lasting that many though it might go on forever. In 1960 a book argued that: *The End of Ideology: On the Exhaustion of Political Ideas in the Fifties*, written by a then famous sociologist, Daniel Bell. This book claimed history here had then reached a plateau, and pretty much ended in this moderate style. It sounded plausible. After all, Eisenhower was a Republican that could push for more regulation of the economy, as with the 1956 Bank Holding Company Act, for instance, which was a major piece of financial regulation of his administration, curbing the worst abuses of Big Money at that time, and giving the Federal Reserve more oversight over its markets, clearly going against "free markets," and government deregulation. The added oversight here was not radical, but it was still a reflection of Big Government responses started under Roosevelt's New Deal, even if it was much moderated so that it was now palatable to almost all of US voters.

Johnson's 1964 Great Society was more left-leaning, and more closely modeled on the "activist government" of the 1930s Big Government, and its New Deal. Johnson's Civil Rights Act was highly egalitarian, trying as it was to eliminate poverty,

---

[101] *https://data.bls.gov/pdq/SurveyOutputServlet*

[102] *https://www.marketwatch.com/story/the-us-economy-will-never-have-another-golden-age-2017-09-01*

much in line with the anti-poverty ideals of the 1930s. It also tried to remove all "barriers to the right to vote," another big egalitarian ideal.[103] Even the later, staunchly conservative Republican President Richard Nixon still launched two Big Government initiatives: the 1970 Environmental Protection Agency (EPA), and the 1971 Occupational and Safety Health Administration, or OSHA, the last Big Government initiatives in America after the 1930s.

Big Government only came to a screeching halt in 1973 with the Oil Shock, when international oil prices quadrupled almost overnight, stalling the US economy, and unleashing a rapidly rising inflation that, at its peak in 1980, reached a high of 14.5%.[104] Unemployment now reached its highest point, going as high as 9%.[105] The Oil Shock here ended America's postwar prosperity, this Golden Age of Capitalism, and this once proud, mobile, and car-owning middleclass society was finally shattered,[106] and, as one writer, John Updike, would put it, it meant "the end of the great American ride."[107]

The mid-1960s and 70s Great Inflation was not the 1930s Great Depression. No thousands of banks and businesses closing; no swaths of middle classes losing their entire savings. No 80% fall in the stock market; no 25% or 30% unemployment rate. The 1970s were painful, shocking, and also lasted for about a decade. But they were no depression,[108]

---

[103] *https://www.britannica.com/event/Great-Society*
http://www.lbjlibrary.org/lyndon-baines-johnson/perspectives-and-essays/seeing-is-believing-the-enduring-legacy-of-lyndon-johnson

[104] *https://www.federalreservehistory.org/essays/great_inflation*

[105] *https://news.gallup.com/poll/9967/timeline-polling-history-events-shaped-united-states-world.aspx*

[106] For a comprehensive data-based study of the uniqueness of this period, see: Gordon, Robert. *The rise and fall of American growth*. Princeton, NJ: Princeton University Press, 2016.

[107] *https://www.marketplace.org/2016/05/31/economy/how-oil-shortage-1970s-shaped-todays-economic-policy*

[108] *https://news.gallup.com/poll/9967/timeline-polling-history-events-shaped-united-*

and very importantly, there was also no major shift to the Left at this time. In fact, the mid-1970s marked an even larger shift to the Right, not to the Left.

Why?

The Oil Shock did not shift public opinion in favor of more government intervention. On the contrary, it made the public mood even more anti-government than before, and under such growing anti-government sentiments, the Left never prospers: it falls apart.

How did this come about?

Short answer: no deflation.

Prices during the 1970s did not collapse, as happens during depressions. On the contrary, prices now rose. Inflation was still possible, even in the midst of the mid-1970s economic doldrums. During the 1970s, the US economy was still *strong enough to avoid a full depression*. But it was not strong enough to avoid *stagnation*. This was the key difference. It was a terrible crux: stagnation *plus* inflation; or *stagflation.*[109] Print more money to stimulate the economy, and you accelerate inflation. Stop printing money, and you leave the economy stagnating. *Damn-if-you-do, damn-if-you-don't*. The government had no way of solving this problem. "Pump up demand, and you pump up prices," as one expert put it. "Try to put a damper on inflation, and you make the recession worse."[110] Either way, government was useless. It could no longer pay its way out of

---

states-world.aspx

[109] *https://www.marketplace.org/2016/05/31/economy/how-oil-shortage-1970s-shaped-todays-economic-policy*
http://mikerazar.com/chart-it/2015/01/08/measuring-the-relationship-between-oil-and-economic-growth/ageconsearch.umn.edu/bitstream/12121/1/wp060029.pdf

[110] *https://www.thebalance.com/opec-oil-embargo-causes-and-effects-of-the-crisis-3305806*
https://www.sanders.senate.gov/newsroom/must-read/economic-trouble-ahead-brattleboro-reformer

this crisis.[111] It also made it look weak. Even President Jimmy Carter admitted this back in 1978, arguing that, "Government cannot solve our problems, it can't set our goals, it cannot define our vision."[112] Ronald Reagan put this lack of power by the government in even clearer terms: "The Most Terrifying Words – *'I'm from the government and I'm here to help.'*" The public soon lost its patience with this borderline useless government, and support for the federal government began to crumble, falling from a high of 80% back in the mid-1960s, to a crushing 25% just two decades later.[113] No surprise then that politics shifted sharply *against the government*, and in favor of anti-government "free enterprise." The Right, of course, began having a field day starting from this point onwards. Its anti-government narrative was now fully vindicated, and "free markets" came back with a vengeance. The opinion polls reflected this. Just between 1973 and 1987, for instance, by one estimate, politics in America shifted to the Right by 14%.[114] The "free market" economist Milton Friedman then became so colossally popular that he even won the 1976 Nobel Prize for economics, solidifying, thus, this born-again "free market" gospel, and apparently this time for all time.

To defeat *stagflation* one had to just allow private capital the freedom to allocate its investments as it preferred, and this market-driven efficiency would then stimulate the economy again by making it more productive, eliminating both inflation

---

[111] *https://www.investopedia.com/articles/investing/110915/review-bernie-sanders-economic-policies.asp*

[112] *https://www.presidency.ucsb.edu/documents/the-state-the-union-address-delivered-before-joint-session-the-congress-1*

[113] *https://www.pewresearch.org/politics/2021/05/17/public-trust-in-government-1958-2021/*

[114] Quoted in: Tuschman, Avi. *Our Political Nature. The Evolution of What Divides Us.* Amherst, NY: Prometheus Books, 2013, p. 51. The highest point of support for government came in 1985. There was another big spike in 1994, perhaps the result of the end of the Cold War.

and stagnation at the *same time*. Two birds with one stone. All that was needed was for the hated government to "free" private capital from all those "stifling" constraints that official regulations had created, and then this now fully free enterprise would take care of the rest.[115]

Public opinion seemed sold on the idea. Polls now showed that private enterprise now had gained new levels of popularity among the public. Only about a quarter of Americans supported private enterprise back in 1973. And just a decade later, by the 1980s, this support now reached almost one third of all Americans.[116]

The year 1979, as one journalist, Christian Caryl, has argued, might be seen as the turning point for public opinion for going anti-government. His book was titled, *Strange Rebels: 1979 and the Birth of the 21st Century*.[117] This year, the year 1979, was when a well-known conservative author, Irving Krystal, published his "Confessions of a true, self-confessed 'neoconservative,'" first coining the term *neoconservative*, later shorted to *neocon*, made this anti-government posture self-affirming, proudly announcing its opposition to the policies of Big Government.[118] The year 1979 was also the year President Carter gave his "Crisis of Confidence" speech on the decaying power of government, and the malaise of this era.[119] The year 1979 was also the first year Democrats began raising money from corporations, much like Republicans had been doing for

---

[115] *https://www.economist.com/blogs/buttonwood/2016/02/economics-and-democracy*

[116] *https://news.gallup.com/poll/1597/confidence-institutions.aspx*

[117] See: Caryl, Christian. *Strange Rebels: 1979 and the Birth of the 21st Century*. New York: Basic Books, 2013.

[118] *https://web.archive.org/web/20121114100459/ http://www.nationalreview.com/articles/206955/neoconservative-invention/jonah-goldberg*

[119] *https://www.npr.org/templates/story/story.php?storyId=106508243 http://www.presidency.ucsb.edu/ws/?pid=32596*

decades, thus blurring the ideological line between these two parties. A "sour and skeptical attitude toward government" now began spreading among voters, as authors Ruy Teixeira and Joel Rogers have also argued. They also pointed out that this was the starting point also of those "deep state" conspiracies, and the rallying of the "White working class" around political stances such as that of bearing arms, a last stand perhaps against the loss of Union power, and their ability to remain relevant in this era of massive industry offshoring, and massive loss of Union jobs. The Democrats, in turn, began putting more energy into immigrant and environmental rights, which the working class began to see as treason to American values. It was now that President Carter lost the working class vote, a huge 55% of the total national vote back then. Worse still, during this failed 1980 reelection bid, much of the working class switched sides, moving towards the Republicans, and especially towards Ronald Reagan: the so-called *Reagan Democrats*. This Republican "White working class" pull was what allowed Reagan's "anti-tax, small-government message" a major win in that year's election.[120] Reagan then proudly proclaimed: "In the present crisis, the government is not the solution to our problem; government *is* the problem."[121] The old 1930s New Deal Big Government ideal was over. The government was now a drag on the economy, even a treacherous force, to be eliminated or at least severely reduced, as would happen decades later with the rise of Donald Trump.

---

[120] In 1980, only 34% of the "White working class" voted for Carter, the reason why Reagan then won by a landslide, carrying all but six states, and the majority of the popular vote (50.7%). See: Ruy Teixeira and Joel Rodgers, *America's Forgotten Majority. Why the White Working Class Still Matters*. New York, NY: Basic Books, 2000, p. 7 and 19.

[121] *https://www.reaganfoundation.org/ronald-reagan/reagan-quotes-speeches/inaugural-address-2/*

Bill Clinton's 1990s North American Free Trade Agreement, or NAFTA, only accelerated the offshoring of industry, further alienating the working class, and probably costing the Democrats many more elections. The Democrat Clinton backed offshoring, austerity, and globalization, killing millions of jobs, accelerating both inequality and deindustrialization. Two years later, Clinton even declared that, "The era of Big Government is over,"[122] thus permanently cutting off the Democrats from the last link they had had with Roosevelt's "activist" government, and its commitment to defend the interests of the many by regulate the economy in favor of fair and egalitarian principles.

The new more cultural approach of Democrats egalitarian or liberal ideals were seen now as performative, especially around championing immigrants, women's and environmental rights, now regarded as extreme, false, or even coercive left-wing identity politics to supposedly address systemic injustices, particularly regarding race, gender, and sexual orientation, it would soon be called *woke ideology*, and become hated by the Right. This portrayal of government as a treasonous force would also be the starting point of the later rightwing populist rise of Donald Trump and his MAGA movement in the 2010s.

This all only accelerated anti-government feelings and the overall shift to the Right. After more than two decades of this shifting away from Big Government, the Democratic Party was now pulling more rich voters in than poorer ones during the 2024 presidential election. Those with high incomes and net worth now favored the Democrat Kamala Harris over the Republican Donald Trump, reversing the traditional class base

---

[122] *https://clintonwhitehouse4.archives.gov/WH/New/other/sotu.html* That same year, both Democrats and Republicans passed a bill deregulating the entire energy industry in California, unanimously. Every last representative voted for it —one of the worst energy price hikes in the state, and the then infamous 1990s California blackouts.

of these parties. *Forbes* magazine even reported that 81 billionaires had publicly backed Harris, compared to only 51 for Trump, while the Pew Research Center found that voters with a four-year degree now favored Harris by 16 points, while those without one favored Trump by 14 points.[123]

Will this unprecedented long shift to the Right ever end? Will America fall into a permanent rightwing trap, and never escape? This long shift to the Right might end, but only until the present cycle in history comes full circle with yet another great depression, and another major shift to the Left, and a switch from today's prevailing anti-government mood to a broadly pro-government one. It has happened before, regularly so, and in all likelihood, will happen again, and perhaps not all that far into the future either, as will be argued in the next two chapters.

---

[123] *https://www.pewresearch.org/politics/2025/06/26/voting-patterns-in-the-2024-election/*
https://eig.org/economic-geography-2024/

3. THE VERY LONG SHIFT TO THE RIGHT

Large economic depressions are cyclical, hitting the US economy every 40 years or so. Forty years after the Depression of 1837, for instance, came the Long Depression, lasting, with some ups and downs, from 1873 until 1893. And 40 or so years after that came the 1930s Great Depression, lasting at least a decade or so. The next depression, following this same cycle, should have hit the US then in 1973 or thereabouts. But this didn't happen. Instead, the economy here "only" saw a decade-long *stagflation,* which was bad, yes, but nowhere near the severe 30% economic contraction seen usually during depressions.[124]

But why was there no depression during the 1970s? The reason for this was mostly *geopolitical.* After World War II, the US rose to become the first truly *global* empire in history, with a prodigious, worldwide control over commerce, finance, and

---

[124] The mid-1970s and early 80s "just" two 3% drops in the US GDP: one between 1973 and 1975; and a second one between 1981 and 1982. *https://www.statista.com/statistics/996758/rea-gdp-growth-united-states-1930-2019/.*

industry, and fueling then the decades of expansion that followed, especially between the 1940s and 1960s, when its economy more than *doubled* in size, and its middle classes became as affluent as they would ever be; and when its largest new generation, the Baby Boomers, also grew to become the most extensive and wealthy of any in US history.[125] No wonder this time was dubbed the "Golden Age of Capitalism."[126] It was unprecedented in affluence, and its exceptional growth saved the country from falling into a depression during the 1970s.

On the whole, this was a good thing. No full-blown decade-long depression, "just" a decade of very ugly stagflation. But with no depression, there was also no major shift to the Left at this time. On the contrary, the US ended up with an unparalleled shift in the *other* direction, towards the Right, starting in the mid-1970s, and unleashing what would then be the longest Right shift in history, one that continues to this day, and which we may call, a bit unimaginatively perhaps, the *Very Long Shift to the Right*. But it should be remembered that this Very Long Shift to the Right has been an *anomaly*. There have been shifts to the Right before, but none lasting more than 20 or 30 years. The 1850s-60s, for instance, saw a big shift to the Right, but it only lasted 20 years or so. And the late-1910s and 1920s also saw a big shift to the Right, but it only lasted 20 years in total. A "normal" shift Right only lasted about two decades. It meant that anti-government sentiments; the "free market," *laissez faire* policies, and deregulation, also usually only lasted for about two decades. After these two decades, an economic *depression* then would hit, reversing public mood, and shifting it once more back to the Left, towards a big push

---

[125] *https://www.investopedia.com/terms/b/baby_boomer.asp*

[126] *https://www.britannica.com/story/americas-boomer-generation* Rates of 4% per year on average, and almost 5% during the 1960s. Marglin, Stephen A., and Juliet B. Schor. *The Golden Age of Capitalism.* Oxford, UK: Clarendon Press, 1991, p. 1.

for more pro-government policies, public spending, consumer protection, assistance programs, and market regulation. This has been a well-established pattern for centuries now. Even as far back as in 1787, Thomas Jefferson had already noticed it, and warned us: "God forbid we should ever be 20 years without such a [popular] rebellion," by which he meant some sort of shift to the Left. Jefferson then added: "What country can preserve its liberties if their rulers are not warned from time to time that their people preserve the spirit of resistance?" His conclusion was the following: "Let them take arms... The tree of liberty must be refreshed from time to time with the blood of patriots & tyrants. It is its natural manure."[127]

But today's situation is very different. Today's shift to the Right has already lasted *more than 50 years*, double the usual length, and with it, American politics have become extremely distorted, leaving us with unprecedented rightwing policies, including an exceptional rise of the far-right, typically a fringe ideology, but that has, nevertheless, now gained almost full control of the federal government under the two terms of President Donald Trump.

This Very Long Shift to the Right also has made the Right *appear* unstoppable, even eternal, including its worship of anti-government sentiments, austerity, and deregulation. Today, market-driven, "free markets," and *laissez faire* polices have become gospel; so much so that today it was nearly "impossible" now to even "imagine" a "coherent alternative" to this rightwing shift, which has become, apparently, "the only viable political and economic system" on the table, as one

[127] Of course, Jefferson envisioned violence for such leftwing shifts, likely because he lived through the American Revolution, and the equally violent 1787 Dutch Revolution, and then France's 1789 Revolution. This refreshing of the tree of liberty, as Jefferson put it, then had to be violent. But history showed that later big shifts to the Left were led by liberal and progressive movements and parties, usually not resorting to violent uprisings. *https://www.loc.gov/exhibits/jefferson/105.html*

philosopher, Mark Fisher, once put it in an aptly named book, *Capitalist Realism: Is There No Alternative?*[128]

The most affected generation by this incredibly long shift to the Right was the Generation X, or GenX, or Americans that came of age in 1984, the first have grown almost completely inside this uniquely super-extended rightwing world. Growing during the mid-1970s stagflation, GenXers also became a particularly *disillusioned* cohort: the least likely to vote; the least likely to be civically engaged; and the least likely to embrace leftwing ideals.[129] Highly individualistic, world-weary, and skeptical, GenXers also became almost "naturally" *libertarian*, a generation that believed, "more in personal freedom than in collective liberation," as a French sociologist, Alain Touraine, once put it.[130]

GenX was also the first generation since World War II to end up worse off economically than their parents.

GenXers also witnessed almost everything shifting to the Right. They witnessed a liberal president, the Democrat Jimmy Carter, pushing for conservative *fiscal* policies, while, at the same time willing to criticize human rights abuses, a balancing act done by an amorphously liberal president that satisfied no one, and that did nothing for the malaise of this era, or to truly help with leftwing causes.

GenXers also saw Carter's successor, the Republican Ronald Reagan, a self-assured, 100% market-driven, smooth-talking candidate rise to win the 1980 election almost in a landslide. Most GenXers saw him then as driven, clear, and, overall, even

---

128 Fisher, Mark. *Capitalist Realism: Is There No Alternative?* Winchester, UK: Zero Books, 2010, p. 2.

129 *https://www.washingtonpost.com/lifestyle/style/we-thought-gen-x-was-a-bunch-of-slackers-now-theyre-the-suits/2017/03/01/eba47346-f924-11e6-9845-576c69081518_story.html*

130 Touraine, Alain. *The return of the actor. Social theory in postindustrial society*, Minneapolis, University of Minnesota Press, 1988, p. 18.

a much more convincing figure.

GenXers also saw Communist China open its economy to global and market-driven principles during the 1980s; they saw Eastern Europe's communism fall in 1989; and the communist Soviet Union, the Evil Empire, dissolve in 1991-92; and the world turn into what seemed an overall acceptance of those individualist, entrepreneurial trends, and their market-driven values, and confirmed anti-government paths as true solutions to society and the economy.

To top this, GenXers also saw America enter in a later rapid economic expansion, the 1990s "boom," or Roaring 90s,[131] lauded then as a "Second Great Age of Global Capitalism," and one more sign, it was said, of a final "triumph of economic liberalism,"[132] and of "capitalism," all, once more, market-driven, and deregulated.[133]

This was when that American political scientist Francis Fukuyama proclaimed the end of history, or as he put it: "not just ... the passing of a particular period of post-war history, but the end of history [itself]... the end-point of mankind's ideological evolution," with a "universalization of Western liberal democracy as the final form of human government."[134] His book was published in 1994, at the dawn of the Roaring 90s, with Fukuyama now seemingly rising as one of its true prophets and true guides for the future.

More importantly perhaps, in 1994 GenXers also witnessed

---

[131] Between 1993 and 2000 there was a 4.5% yearly growth, and a record low 4% unemployment. *https://www.brookings.edu/research/retrospective-on-american-economic-policy-in-the-1990s*

[132] Gordon, *op. cit.*, p. 529.

[133] GenXers also saw that same year the publication of the first salient novel describing their own generation, Prozac Nation, by Elizabeth Wurtzel, who focused on individualized struggles against depression, suicide, and drug abuse, embarking then on an equally individualized path towards recovery.

[134] Fukuyama, Francis. "The End of History?" in *The National Interest*, no. 16, 1989, pp. 3–18. *http://www.jstor.org/stable/24027184*

the worst congressional flip against the Democratic Party *in 40 years*, when this party lost 54 congressional seats in just one single swoop, a terrible loss for the Left.[135]

In 1994 a new, rising leader of the Republican Party, Newt Gingrich, also published his anti-government book, *Contract with America*, calling for sweeping cuts to government, taxes, and welfare.[136]

The year 1994 was also the year President Bill Clinton, a Democrat, paradoxically perhaps, signed into law the North American Free Trade Agreement, or NAFTA, a massive betrayal of America's working class, killing millions of manufacturing jobs, and accelerating inequality and deindustrialization, with Clinton later even declaring that, "The era of Big Government is over,"[137] thus succumbing then fully to the overall anti-government sentiment embraced now also by the Democrats.

Finally, the year 1994 was the year when the book *The Bell Curved* appeared, "proving" statistically and "scientifically" that inequality was supposedly the result, in part at least, of a "natural" order, where the more intelligent "cognitive elite" rose over the rest as the result of inherited, environmental factors, including "race."

Born to this kind of rightwing world, GenXers seemed to find little choice other than to embrace "capitalism," with many also admiring the individualist libertarian author Ayn Rand, and her novels where individualists were the heroes, and the collectivist characters were always villains.

The next generation to grow up in America, the Millennials

---

[135] *https://history.house.gov/Institution/Majority-Changes/Majority-Changes/*

[136]*https://web.archive.org/web/20100323102923/http://www.heritage.org/Research/Lecture/The-Contract-with-America-Implementing-New-Ideas-in-the-US*

[137] *https://clintonwhitehouse4.archives.gov/WH/New/other/sotu.html* That same year, both Democrats and Republicans passed a bill deregulating the entire energy industry in California, unanimously. Every last representative voted for it —one of the worst energy price hikes in the state, and the infamous 1990s California blackouts.

(born 1981–1996) currently the largest voting-age generation, had a different experience. Experts describe this generation as "political explorers," who took now an "à la carte" approach to voting, giving their support to more specific policies rather to a full party platform.[138] The youngest of them were about 27 years-old when the second worst economic downturn in 70 years hit the US: the 2008 Global Financial Crisis, or *Great Recession.* This recession cut America's GDP by more than 4%, sending unemployment to almost 10%, the highest in 25 years.[139] It also left 10 million Americans out of their homes,[140] while the top 1% only got richer, and the rest significantly poorer.[141] It's true that even after this massive crash, most Millennials still did not abandon the old anti-government ideals in vogue since the mid-1970s. Millennials voters felt betrayed, disenfranchised, and angry, even scared.[142] And after the 2008 crisis, voters then hit the polls with a vengeance, resulting in the highest turnout in the country in 40 years.[143] And this time they elected a moderate president, the Democrat Barak Obama; a somewhat center-left, outsider figure; a middle-grounder that, in the end, would leave many disappointed. He pursued a major healthcare reform, yes, but also continued with the old and strong pro-business policies of his predecessors, and bailed out the Big Banks, the same ones that had caused the 2008 recession in the first place. To many in the Left, this was then a "missed" opportunity, or as the

---

[138] *https://www.pewresearch.org/politics/2018/03/01/the-generation-gap-in-american-politics/*

[139] *https://www.brookings.edu/research/nine-facts-about-the-great-recession-and-tools-for-fighting-the-next-downturn/*

[140] *www.nytimes.com/2009/06/01/opinion/01krugman.html*

[141] *https://www.factcheck.org/2016/03/clinton-sanders-bailout-brawl/*

[142] *https://www.brookings.edu/research/nine-facts-about-the-great-recession-and-tools-for-fighting-the-next-downturn/*

[143] *http://www.washingtonpost.com/wp-dyn/content/article/2008/12/14/AR2008121402295.html*

British sociologist William Davis once put it, Obama had "originally excited the left," but soon saw him turn into a "coup for finance capital."[144]

Millennials then combined Left views, but with some Right views, too. A majority (57%) held liberal views on social issues, particularly regarding LGBTQ+ acceptance, and even on the benefits of immigration. They supported also health care reform, a big form of government intervention. Here, they leaned Left. But at the same time, they still remained skeptical of overall government efficiency, remaining trapped, it seemed, between many liberal inclinations, but also still with a deep-seated distrust for the government, especially in the area of the economy. They disliked the Big Banks, yes, but also the government, and in some cases even more so. So in spite of the growing presence of Millennial voters, anti-government sentiments still remained strong. The polls showed this: the approval rates of Big Banks, for instance, took a tough beating with the 2008 crisis, falling from 75% to a low of 45% by 2017.[145] And support for "free markets" fell also at this time, from a high of 80% *before* 2008, to just 59% in 2017. Among lower-income voters (those making less than $30,000 a year) this support for "free markets" fell at *twice* the speed than with the rest of the population, reaching a low of 44% —a record low for any segment of the population.[146] Clearly, the 2008 crisis had not been able to stop end the anti-government

---

[144] Davis, William. "Destination Unknown," in *London Review of Books*, June 9, 2022, p. 15.

[145]Disapproval for big banks also rose to a record 30% after 2008, at par only with very unpopular US industries like Big Oil, and Big Pharma.
http://news.gallup.com/poll/192719/americans-confidence-banks-languishing-below.aspx
http://news.gallup.com/poll/12748/business-industry-sector-ratings.aspx
http://freakonomics.com/2011/03/09/mistrust-and-the-great-recession/

[146] *https://www.huffingtonpost.com/2011/04/07/us-china-brazil-free-market-support_n_846169.html*

sentiments among most voters. Big Banks might have done poorly at this time, but the federal government did *even worse*, with its approval rates here remaining as low as 20% or 25% by 2017,[147] almost half the rate enjoyed by the Big Banks. Worse still for the Left, in later years, it was the banks that recovered much of their approval, and not the federal government.[148]

How could any liberal-inspired politician then go after the Big Bad Banks if the public disliked the government even more than the banks? With no backing from polls, what chance did they have at pushing through effective legislation to stop them?

This paralyzed leftwing politics. In fact, this has been paralyzing the Left since the mid-1970s: a persistent anti-government feeling that will not allow full-fledge policies to go break up near-monopolies or oligopolies, and curb the ever-rising inequality.[149]

The Right, in contrast, fully benefitted from this anti-government sentiment. And it was also now being super-charged by ever larger funding coming from the super-rich. The new 2010 *Citizens United* Supreme Court now allowed corporations to spend *unlimited* amounts of money on political candidates, usually rightwing, or far-right ones, a decision that accelerated more this anti-government mood and rightwing

---

[147] *http://www.people-press.org/2015/11/23/1-trust-in-government-1958-2015/* *http://news.gallup.com/poll/12748/business-industry-sector-ratings.aspx*

[148] America's top three banks also went on to add $2.4 trillion dollars to domestic accounts between 2008 and 2018, a whopping 180% rise. *https://www.wsj.com/articles/biggest-three-banks-gobble-up-2-4-trillion-in-new-deposits-since-crisis-1521711001* According to financial columnist Rana Foroohar, banks only made 7% of the economy, yet took "almost a quarter of corporate profits." Foroohar, Rana. "The Dangers of Financialization" (video). Interview, Oct. 11, 2016. *https://www.youtube.com/watch?v=vtlk7WlINPQ* *http://www.tandfonline.com/doi/abs/10.1080/13563467.2017.1311850*

[149] Voters still remained very anti-government, with one poll finding that most in 2015 still stood against a more "government-managed economy," at 66%. Less than a third supported a more "government-managed economy. *http://reason.com/blog/2015/02/12/poll-americans-like-free-markets-more-t2*

candidates. It caused a veritable avalanche of undisclosed "dark money" for rightwing and far-right causes, as journalist Jane Mayer argued in her book, *Dark Money: The Hidden History of the Billionaires Behind the Rise of the Radical Right*,[150] and it was also no surprise then that after 2010 far-right groups (extreme nationalist, xenophobic, and homophobic, and those from fundamentalist religious groups) started winning an unprecedented number of elections, and going from a fringe group, to a mainstream presence in the country. *Citizens United*, plus the 2008 crisis, was the cocktail that looped donor and publically-elected officials and accelerated the nexus between the super-rich and the far-right, feeding ever bigger political donors, and ever more rightwing policies, ending with the two wins of President Donald Trump in 2016 and in 2024.

Citizens United (plus the 2008 crisis) seemed to have fueled this accelerated far-right, as can be seen in the following suggestive examples:

- Since the 2010 *Citizens United* decision, there was a major rise of hate groups —almost all far-right—which, within just seven years, saw these groups multiply by a factor of *seven*.[151]
- Right after *Citizens United* decision, Democrats also suffered an absolutely massive congressional flip against them, this during the 2010 midterm elections, with Democrats here losing, in one single swoop, 63 seats in Congress, their worst congressional flip against

---

150 *https://www.cnn.com/2014/02/27/politics/tea-party-greatest-hits/index.html https://www.newyorker.com/magazine/2021/08/09/the-big-money-behind-the-big-lie*

151 Increase between 2008 and 2015. *Hate groups* advocate hatred or violence towards any race, ethnicity, nation, religion, sex, or gender. Before 2008, the US "only" had 149 such groups. By 2015, there were already 998. See: Johnson, Daryl. *Hateland. A Long, Hard Look at America's Extremist Hart.* Amherst, NY; Prometheus Books, 2019, p. 25.

them *in 100 years!*[152]

- Just six years right after the 2010 *Citizens United* decision, a suspicious *and* alarming jump of 22% happened in the levels of corruption in the US, according to a study in the magazine *Foreign Policy*.[153]

The Left also did reasonably well during this time. *Occupy Wall Street* protests, for instance, spread nationally, and even internationally, focusing on inequality, and on rising money-influence on politics, and on a new and well-received slogan, *We are the 99%*, highlighting the widening chasm in society between the haves and the have nots.

But the far-right Tea Party movement did even better. Using outsider candidates, too, it had an even clearer, more streamlined anti-government message, also better suited for the times. Simple and clear cut: *cut taxes; shrink the government*; the Tea Party went on to gain a much larger representation in the US Congress, forming then the 2015 far-right congressional Freedom Caucus, aiming at accelerating more their radical causes within the Republican Party, which soon became mostly far-right.

---

[152] *https://history.house.gov/Institution/Majority-Changes/Majority-Changes/* The Left fought back bank bailouts with the 2011 Occupy Wall Street protests. But Occupy Wall Street didn't have the pizazz of the rightwing Tea Party. Its message was heart-felt, but too low specifics and directness.
https://www.onthecommons.org/tea-party-vs-occupy-wall-street
https://www.cnn.com/2021/01/16/politics/insurrection-investigation-washington-lockdown/index.html
https://crisislex.org/papers/sss16-camera-ready.pdf
https://newrepublic.com/article/153122/missing-black-millennial The almost 100-member hodgepodge of liberals, progressives, and socialists in the Congress Progressive Caucus was also less effective at capitalizing discontent compared to the rightwing Freedom Caucus at pressuring for more radical policies.
https://www.nytimes.com/2021/10/01/us/politics/progressive-democrats-infrastructure.html

[153] This between 2015 and 2021. *https://foreignpolicy.com/2021/01/28/report-transparency-international-corruption-worst-decade-united-states/*

But the unique *internal makeup* of the Republican Party was another factor in the rise of the far-right.

Republicans were *always* a vastly more radical party than the Democrats.

Among *all* American voters, the far-right (mostly rightwing populists, and Christian nationalists) constituted only about 22% of the total population, a minority that had never really enjoyed a true *national* power. But *within the Republican Party*, the far-right's influence has always been very considerable, with almost half of all Republicans here being far-right. Until 2010, the Republican mainstream had mostly been able to constrain its far-right. But after the 2008 crisis, and the 2010 *Citizens United* and its the rapid rise of "dark money," the far-right suddenly gained unprecedented strength, soon rising to become *the* decisive force in the Republican Party. It was now Trump saw his unprecedented rapid rise to the top. Having betted on the far-right early on, after *Citizens United*, an outsider like Trump took the lead in rightwing politics, gaining, in 2016, the nomination, then, after winning the presidential elections that year, also won the presidency. Trump was then able to cleanse the entire GOP of its moderates (branded now as *Republicans In Name Only*, or RINOS), and turn it into a MAGA-exclusive force under his sole and highly centralized leadership.[154]

The far-left (progressives, socialists, and greens) *never* had any comparable chance of taking over the Democratic Party in any similar way. Democrats were always *structurally* moderate. *Within* this party, the far-left constituted only *about*

[154] Trump here broke off this party from its 1980s Reagan's conservative roots, and re-built it now as an almost purely populist force. "Is its patron saint Ronald Reagan or Donald Trump?" as *The Wall Street Journal* wondered. *https://www.wsj.com/articles/can-the-gop-become-a-real-working-class-party-11674835143*

a quarter of its total force,[155] and such a small proportion was *never* enough to take over the entire party. Perhaps the outsider Bernie Sanders, from the far-left, may have been the candidate most voters wanted in the Left; the one that could fill stadiums; inject true enthusiasm in his followers. He might have even beaten Trump in 2016. Who knows? But he couldn't pull off anything like the coup Trump achieved in the Republican Party; much less eject all moderate elements from this party, and then turn it into a far-left centralized, militant force that would exclusively follow his own democratic socialist, progressive, and green inclinations. The aparatchiks of the Democratic Party were able then to stop Sander's path here from taking off almost from the get-go. But this has been the approach of the Democrats since at least the 1970s: try to appeal to the most voters by using moderate candidates. Since the 1970s, the most Democrats could aspire was to slow down the far-right tsunami. Over and over, Democrats have then selected the most lackluster, blandest, and brutally uninspiring candidates they could possibly find, the likes, say, of Hillary Clinton and Kamala Harris,[156] which hardly ever thrilled left-leaning voters, at least not with the same zeal as the far-right was excited to follow Donald Trump.

The Democrats were, at most, resisting the worst excesses

---

[155] US self-described moderates were 34% to 37%. Add Stressed Sideliners (15%); the Ambivalent Right (12%); Outsider Left (10%); plus Establishment Liberals (13%), and Democratic Mainstays (16%), and this moderate core were a handy 66% majority. The more radical Pro-Trump populists, and Faith & Flaggers combined constituted 22% of voters, almost the same as Stressed Sideliners (15%); the Ambivalent Right. Progressives and socialists, the hard-core Bernie fans, barely added 10% of the electorate. Pew Research Institute in:
https://www.themainemonitor.org/are-you-conservative-liberal-or-moderate/
http://news.gallup.com/poll/201152/conservative-liberal-gap-continues-narrow-tuesday.aspx

[156] Since 2021, support for a more moderate party has grown by 11 percentage points, reaching 45%, among Democrats and Democratic-leaning independents.
https://news.gallup.com/poll/656636/democrats-favor-party-moderation-past.aspx

of the Right. What else could they do? The super-rich and the Right have been on the *offensive* since the mid-1970s; and the far-right has been on the ascendancy since the 2010s. The Right was then the one with the *initiative*. Democratic presidents like Clinton, Obama, or Biden were, at best, *speed-bumps* in an otherwise accelerating shift to the Right since the 1970s. The Right and the rich were the ones winning now. As investor Warren Buffett once put it: "There's class warfare, all right, but it's my class, the rich class, that's making war."[157] The job of the Democrats then has been to hold on, perhaps to seek protect whatever pieces of public assistance, Social Security, Medicare, and Medicaid they can. In this sense, the Democrats had not done the worst job possible. And at least they still existed.

In contrast, Trump's unbridled enthusiasm has inspired his far-right base to no end, even if he hadn't always commanded a proper national majority, or even maintained the highest approval rates.[158] He still gave the far-right a voice, a unity, and a presence they hadn't had for two centuries. No wonder they loved him as a hero; an idol, a miracle, and as a true *godsend*. No wonder he could do *no* wrong; and no wonder they would *never* let him go. This was their moment of glory. They hadn't been this powerful for the last 200 years. And Trump took them there. He was then the most powerful figure of this age.

But was this *necessarily* the result of an overall change of the country's voting structure, or was it more the result of the Very Long Shift to the Right, now passing the 50-year mark, and delivering to us a fully mobilized far-right, able now to take more or less over the whole of national politics?

---

[157] *https://markets.businessinsider.com/news/stocks/warren-buffett-right-class-war-taxes-rich-bernie-sanders-2020-8-1029532804*

[158] *https://www.nytimes.com/2022/07/11/us/politics/biden-approval-polling-2024.html*
https://www.vox.com/2019/8/21/20813864/experts-recession-trumps-election-2020

The far-right has always been there. It has always been a huge power within the Republican Party. This hasn't changed, not in the last half century, and likely even in the last century or two. Was Trump then *the* change, or just a symptom of a deeper change? If voting blocks of America have not changed, then today's difference was not likely to be found in these blocks, but more likely in the extremely long shift to the Right we see today, which has also kept voter sentiment deeply anti-government, and rendered the Left then unable to launch any consistent effort to use the government as a tool to curb the power of the oligopolies and near monopolies. This is what has then left the oligopolies and near monopolies to roam freely, and fund this unprecedented rise of the Right, and then far-right.

Today's far-right politics are *unprecedented.* Only the 1820s and 30s, with President Andrew Jackson came close to today's Very Long Shift to the Right. And this shift under Jacksonian only lasted 30 years. In contrast, today's Very Long Shift of the Right has lasted more than 50 years; almost double the shift to the Right under Jackson's. And the difference shows. Jackson *only* enjoyed a House-Senate-Presidency trifecta for his first two years in office only. His remainder six years, Congress remained staunchly against him, as did the Supreme Court, blunting his rightwing policies, and frustrating his efforts to push even further to the Right. But Trump has benefited now of a 50-year old shift to the Right, gaining, thus, a *six year* House-Senate-Presidency trifecta, *three times longer* than that of Jackson's. One might even call Trump today a *Jackson on steroids.* It is this difference why it's been so hard to forecast how further the country may still go to the Right. Since we've never lived through such a long Right shift, we have then only a very limited precedent for guessing at what might happen next.

Where will politics head to in the future then?
As absurd as it might sound, America is still a very moderate place. It's true that a full third of US voters today felt that *violence against the government was sometimes justified*, as *The Washington Post* found in a 2017 poll.[159] But even with all this radicalism, and even taste for violence, Americans were still mostly a moderate lot. Most even self-identified as *moderates*, either rightwing or leftwing. So where did all this radicalism come from? Well, from the Very Long Shift to the Right, but also from voters having *absolutely no influence on national politics* anymore. The bottom 70% of voters had *no say in federal politics* at all, as a recent Princeton University study found.[160] Could the US then even call itself a democracy anymore? Not likely. And voters were now turning radical because they were excluded from federal politics. They were not even *represented* here.

Take the *Sanders-Trump voters*, or 12% of the total national vote in 2016 and in 2020, a not insignificant number. They *first* voted for socialist Bernie Sanders, and only *after* Sanders was sidelined, did they switch sides, and voted then for far-right Donald Trump.[161] Were they completely bonkers? Not likely. More likely, they were being *tactical* with their votes, swinging first Left, and then Right in order to pry open a system that no longer represented them. They were using their vote then in the best way they could to make their voices heard. It illogical *ideologically*, but it was subverting the system *tactically*; shaking it up to gain representation at the federal level. They were probably moderate. But they did want to *punish* now a system that no longer worked for them. It wasn't necessarily

159 *https://www.theguardian.com/us-news/2022/jan/02/one-three-americans-violence-government-justified-poll*

160 *https://www.bbc.com/news/blogs-echochambers-27074746*

161 *https://www.washingtonpost.com/news/monkey-cage/wp/2017/08/24/did-enough-bernie-sanders-supporters-vote-for-trump-to-cost-clinton-the-election/*

crazy, at least given the *total* lack of access to power that this bottom 70% now have.

Again, this radicalism was not necessarily *ideological*, but more likely *tactical*. Core ideals here weren't necessarily changing, but the voters were, becoming ever more radical.

Here are some examples of how this *ideologically* moderate core was still setting limits to the supposedly "unstoppable" rise of the far-right today:

- *Abortion*. More than two-thirds of Americans are in favor of "women having access to legal abortion for any reason," as *The Wall Street Journal* found in 2022.[162] This flew in the face of the recent overturning of *Roe vs. Wade*, banning all abortions. According to *The Wall Street Journal*, more than half of American voters also said that, "the issue [of the ban on abortions] made them more likely to cast ballots in the [2022] midterm elections," and mostly *against* the Right.[163]
- *The Supreme Court*. A record-high 42% of Americans now saw this court as too conservative. The Court's approval ratings here have then fallen, and quickly, especially since the 2021 overturning of *Roe vs. Wade*, with such rates dropping from 49% in 2021, to 40% in 2022 —a *nine* percentage point drop in less than a year, its lowest approval rate in *50 years*! Again, voters were still moderates.[164] A later push by conservative judges

[162] *https://www.wsj.com/articles/upholding-roe-v-wade-is-supported-by-most-americans-wsj-poll-finds-11654162200*

[163] Americans that opposed the ban on 6-week and 15-week abortions were also less likely to vote for pro-life candidates. *https://www.wsj.com/articles/support-for-legalized-abortion-grows-since-dobbs-ruling-wsj-poll-shows-11662210020*
https://www.economist.com/united-states/2022/11/11/where-abortion-was-on-the-ballot-americans-voted-to-protect-it
https://news.gallup.com/poll/645836/record-share-electorate-pro-choice-voting.aspx

[164] *https://news.gallup.com/poll/402044/supreme-court-trust-job-approval-historical-lows.aspx*

to ban abortion pills also backfired, hurting the Court's approval rates even more.[165]

- *Gun control*. Most Americans (62%) in 2016 —and 84% of Democrats— were still dissatisfied with the current gun laws, the highest such disapproval rate in 23 years, showing how this moderate core still had a strong grasp on this issue, and had not just given it away to the far-right.[166]
- *The military*. Confidence in the military fell from 70% in 2018, to just 48% in 2022, a stunning and rapid drop, with almost half of those polled here citing the presence of right-wing extremists in the military as the main reason for this faltering support.[167] Fewer Americans wanted to join the military, perhaps also due to this far-right overrepresentation.[168] Although the weak labor market of the late-2020s has pushed many more to join the military since they couldn't find any jobs in the civilian economy.
- *Far-right shock groups*. Leaked chats from one far-right

---

[165] *https://www.nytimes.com/2023/04/10/us/supreme-court-abortion-pill-fda.html* *The New York Times* in 2023: "Pressured by Their Base on Abortion, Republicans Strain to Find a Way Forward;" might even face "dire electoral consequences" in 2024, and even "urging compromise," not just around abortion, but also around "guns and gay rights" by alienating so many moderates. *https://www.nytimes.com/2023/04/11/us/politics/abortion-republicans-elections.html*

[166] Attitudes changed particularly after the 2012 mass shooting at the Newtown, elementary school in Connecticut, when 20 six and seven year-olds were shot dead, plus six adults. *https://news.gallup.com/poll/470588/dissatisfaction-gun-laws-hits-new-high.aspx* *https://news.gallup.com/poll/653489/majorities-back-stricter-gun-laws-assault-weapons-ban.aspx*

[167] *https://www.wsj.com/articles/americans-are-losing-trust-in-the-military-reagan-institute-survey-11669848047*

[168] Infiltrated for decades by rightwing extremists, today's armed forces play a central role in shifting it to the Right. Far-right groups were now "overrepresented" by veterans, active-duty military personnel, and law enforcement; 25% of extremist paramilitary group members had a "military background." *https://www.nytimes.com/2022/11/13/opinion/us-police-military-extremism.html*

group, the Patriot Front, showed its leaders constantly worried about low membership. "We are absolutely desperate for new people," said one such internal email. "We've been in the 220's to 230's membership rut for nearly a full year." Interestingly, the Patriot Front was responsible for 80% of White supremacist incidents in 2020, and this in spite of only having 230 members total.[169] It suggested such groups may be more propaganda than any solid social movement.

- *Immigration*. Voters in mid-2025, suddenly, became "markedly more positive" towards immigration, as a Gallup poll found, with 79% saying that immigration was, "a good thing for the country," a startlingly level of moderation in the face of the staunch anti-immigrant stances unleashed at this time by Trump.[170]
- *Working-class voters*. Republicans recently (2023) captured more than half of all the *lowest*-income House districts, according to the Census, while Democrats took more than half of its *wealthiest* districts, an inversion of the usual class order for the Left. But this inversion came at a price. The Right now had created a new tension for itself, making it harder for Republicans to keep cutting Medicaid, and other safety nets on which low-income voters depended, as *The Wall Street Journal* argued. [171] Trump's second term radical anti-government policies as outlined in *Project 2025* benefited corporate and capital gain taxes.[172] But won't these reforms affect his own base, which was now

---

[169] *https://www.theguardian.com/world/2022/jan/28/leaked-online-chats-white-nationalist-patriot-front*

[170] *https://news.gallup.com/poll/692522/surge-concern-immigration-abated.aspx*

[171] *https://www.wsj.com/politics/the-problematic-politics-of-trumps-bill-more-lower-income-americans-are-voting-gop-0b6288d0*

[172] *https://www.project2025.org/*

increasingly low-income? A former far-right White House strategist, Steve Bannon, argued that a split between elites and the wider Trump MAGA base might break this unity.[173]

- *ICE*. The aggressive use of ICE agents in Minneapolis soon led to a massive outcry in this city supported by the vast majority of moderate voters in the country, and that led to Trump's administration having to withdraw the vast majority of this force.
- *Greenland*. Trump's efforts to seize Greenland from Denmark in 2025 also faced a majority of Americans opposing it, and he also had to give up on this effort.
- *Elections*. Trump's idea to nationalize or federalize the upcoming elections found the Republican heads of the Senate and the House both immediately opposing it.
- *Tariffs*. The 2026 Supreme Court ruling against emergency-based trade completely undermined what Trump had argued had the legal authority to do since 2025.

But would this moderate American voter core mean that the far-right would not be able then to take over the entire country permanently into the future?

That is a key question: how far could the far-right still go? Again, given the exceptionally long shift the Right today, this was hard to forecast.

So let's go by parts.

Today's Very Long Shift to the Right, the longest in history, was not completely unprecedented *in its nature*. It was unique in its length, yes, but big shifts to the Right had happened before, in particular under President Andrew Jackson in the

[173] *https://www.nytimes.com/2025/07/01/podcasts/the-daily/steve-bannon-interview-maga.html*

1820s and 30s. And the parallels between Jackson's time and our own were remarkable, and also at least somewhat significant to make such forecasts. Jackson 1820s-30s rightwing populist push, for instance, turned the executive into a powerful, nationalist office, championing the "common white man," a strong parallel with today's Trump's drive to shift power away from established, educated elites, and use the presidential veto to expand his own authority just as Jackson had done. Trump also used this power to override Congress and the Supreme Court, also just as Jackson.

Jackson also redefined the US presidency on the 1820s-30s, acting as the sole representative of the people; yet again, much like with Trump today. And then Jackson also attacked the Second Bank of the United States as a government-backed monopoly favoring the wealthy. Again a certain parallel with Trump's here was also suggestive, with his current attacks on the Federal Reserve System, America's new central bank, which he viewed as equally opaque, negative, and deceptive for the economy.

In 1830, Jackson also signed the Indian Removal Act, authorizing the US federal government to force the relocation of Native-American tribes from the southeastern US to lands west of the Mississippi River. It was a brutal policy, and Jackson here ignored a Supreme Court ruling prohibiting it, which again, sounded much like Trump's accelerated policy of today of forcefully removing immigrants from the US, also done in spite of various court rulings against it, and which Trump has also ignored.

Jackson also protected slavery, and viewed abolitionists as threats. The 1820s-30s then became an era of many attacks against such abolitionists, the Black Lives Matter of the time. In 1834, for instance, New York City saw large anti-abolition riots; and in Washington DC in 1835, riots broke out targeting free Black residents, the so called "Snow-storm" riots. A series of riots also broke out throughout northern US in 1835, including in Boston, and also targeting abolitionists. They were later dubbed the "Gentleman's" Riots. Very much in parallel, Trump has repeatedly and publically criticized Black Lives Matter protests, particularly during 2020, and it was then that some in the far-right attacked such peaceful demonstrations, including when a Virginia Ku Klux Klan leader intentionally drove his truck into such a crowd. Trump then framed the incident as Black Lives Matters protesters as the ones being the violent, divisive force here, calling them a radical threat to "law and order." Both the 1820s-30s Jackson, and the 2010s-20s Trump then had in common this conservative, exclusionary focus of consolidating power for "white males." Trump's current cutbacks on the Diversity, Equity, and Inclusion, or DEI programs (strategies that sought to foster fair representation and sense of belonging for all individuals, particularly from historically marginalized groups) also seemed to mimic Jackson's push for power for "white males" in the 1820s-30s, constituting yet another parallel between the two.

Jackson also used his personal popularity during the 1820s and 30s to build a new political party structure, much like Trump today also, and also using his popularity to purge and reshape his Republican Party from the RHINOS, expelling anyone who might oppose him. Trump then also turned this party into a personalized political tool only for dedicated followers, loyal only to him. Here Jackson and Trump seem to follow another strong authoritarian parallel. It should also be mentioned that, although labeled the "Jacksonian Democracy" era, making it sound democratic, Jackson was in reality a "democratic autocrat," which could perhaps also be said about Trump today.

Also interestingly, Jackson's era was among the most violent in American history, even dubbed at times the "Republic of Violence," since it saw more than 50 major, distinct incidents of rioting just in 1834 and 1835 alone. One newspaper from that time summarized it all in the following manner: "there has never been a time like this," with "rumor after rumor of riot, insurrection, and tumult."[174] One might then also draw a parallel between this time and today's equally intense protest during the January 6th, 2020 attack on the Washington DC Capitol Building, one that forced the evacuation of all its personnel, and resulting in some deaths, and in over 140 injuries to law enforcement, and also in roughly $1.5 million in damages.

The violence of Jackson's era also fueled a growing anti-immigrant ideology favoring established, native-born inhabitants over newcomers, and ideology that in Jackson's time was known as Nativism. It was these Nativist-inspired riots that in the 1830s regularly targeted abolitionists, Black citizens, and minority groups, and Irish Catholic immigrants, back then the more recent arrivals. Again, it all seemed to parallel so much with today's anti-Mexican or anti-Somali sentiments, but fueled this time by MAGA sentiments.

Also, Jackson's 1830s led to violent confrontations between the government, and workers. Federal troops, for instance, were used in 1834 to suppress an important labor riot at a major 19th-century waterway transportation project, the Chesapeake and Ohio Canal construction. And in 1835, federal troops were also used to break up a Baltimore bank riot. And in 1837, New York's state militia was used to put down what might have been the most serious riot from this era, New York City's "Flour Riot," a protest born from poverty and rising food costs, which saw a crowd of roughly 6,000 people take to the

---

[174] Quoted in: Fraser, Caroline. *Prairie Fires. The American Dreams of Laura Ingalls Wilder.* New York, NY: Metropolitan Books, 2017, p. 33-34.

streets, driven mainly by hunger and the belief that merchants were hoarding supplies, and then storming a warehouse, breaking into barrels, and dumping all the flour on the street. A parallel could be drawn also with today's inflation and rising inequality, and rise of support for Unions, and an increase in the number of strikes.

Finally, another parallel could be the 1820s-30s racialization of America's Left. Back then, the Equal Rights Party, later called the Locofocos, was a radical splinter group from the then Democratic Party, and it advocated more strongly for working-class interests, and for the abolition of monopolies and chartered banks which they saw as ruining the democracy of this era. They also feared that corrupt Democrats and special corporate privileges were taking over, much like with today's Democratic Socialists, which are equally worried democracy today might be at risk, or even at an end, and were thus radicalizing and distinguishing themselves ever more from more mainstream Democrats.

So, what ended this far-right 1820s-30s era? A rise of the Left. No really. At least not directly. *Only* the Depression of 1837 ended the Jacksonian era. Only then, with this depression, did the public finally shift to the Left, embrace government regulation, and end the authoritarian, rightwing Jacksonian era, and give way then to the sudden triumph of the far more left-leaning Whig Party during the 1840s. And it was the Whigs here that then sent politics in the opposite direction: towards more public investment; more liberal views; and more help for the needy.

The question here then would be if the today's Very Long Shift to the Right might also end then with another depression?

If the answer here is *no*, and that there will be no more depressions, then today's shift to the Right might go on forever. Who knows?

But if there answer is *yes,* then the next question would be when would this depression come and hit the US economy?

4. IS THE END NIGH?

History shows that economic depressions hit in cycles, every 40 or 50 years or so, a pattern that has held true, it seems, for the last 4,000 years. We even see signs of this pattern in ancient texts, with the Babylonians, for instance, forgiving all debts regularly every 50 years, likely to offset severe economic downturns, or depressions, also in ancient times. Copying the Babylonians, the Hebrew Bible also had a debt forgiveness cycle, in *Leviticus*, also hitting about every 49 to 50 years called *jubilees*, and also likely put in place to ease major downturns in their economy.[175] Japan also had debt forgiveness decrees issued on a regular basis. Known as *tokusei*, or "good government," these dated back to at least 2,300 years, although the *tokusei* didn't happen every half a century, as with the Babylonians.[176] A *tokusei* was only issued after large natural or human-made calamities. But such calamities, it seems, might

---

175 *https://money.howstuffworks.com/personal-finance/debt-management/rolling-jubilee1.htm*

176 Brown, Delmer M. "The Japanese Tokusei of 1297," in *Harvard Journal of Asiatic Studies*, vol. 12, no. 1/2, 1949, pp. 188–206. *https://doi.org/10.2307/2718207*

have hit Japan, on average, every 40 years or so, much like the same 40 to 50-year cycle found in the ancient Middle East.[177]

Such 40 to 50-year cycles still exist today, in modern times, and sometimes referred to as "supercycles," to help to distinguish them from the shorter "business cycles," which hit an economy typically every 3 to 7 years, and which are also better known since they happen several times within a single lifetime, and are then challenges that most of us have had to contend with from time to time. The "supercycles," in contrast, only hit about once every half a century or so, and thus usually catch most societies almost completely unprepared.

The first famous "supercycle" in modern history was perhaps Holland's *tulipmania*, a massive financial bubble that burst in 1637, and that also led to a massive financial collapse, and a decade-long depression, sinking Europe into extreme hardship for the whole of the 1640s. This depression also had a *political* effect, that of shifting European politics to the Left in a major way; a pattern seen for all depressions in the last 400 years. The 1640s then saw major popular uprisings, the most salient example of which was the 1642–1651 English Civil War; a conflict where the English Parliament, in a major anti-monarchical push, executed King Charles I. England at this time even became then *the* hotbed of egalitarian movements in Europe (not yet called *the Left*, as we do today, but that were similar in overall spirit to what we would now call *the Left*), top amongst them being the Levellers who sought to achieve complete egalitarian changes via parliamentary and legal reforms. And then came the Diggers, which sought more locally-based, direct types agrarian forms of what we would now call local cooperativism or socialism. These radical times didn't last forever, though. As the depression ran out of steam,

---

[177] *https://ourworldindata.org/natural-disasters*

and the economy recovered, the egalitarian, anti-monarchical radicalism of the era began to wane, particularly by the late 1850s. But even here, such radicalism still showed its strong influence with the rise in 1651 of the Quakers, another very egalitarian movement, but one now operating under a more personal, and *spiritual* brand of egalitarianism, more based on religious ideals of freedom and pacifism than of widespread social reforms and civil strife. These more personal forms of egalitarian though also fit better with this later, more waning spirit of radicalism during the 1650s.

The following large "supercycle" to hit Europe came half a century later or so, in 1672, leading to yet one more massive financial crisis, the *London Banking Crisis*, when the English economy crashed so bad the English King himself, Charles II, had to default on his debts. This then led to all gold-based banks in the City of London falling into insolvency, and many into permanent closure. The crash was so massive it led to a decade-long depression, and, once again, to a massive shift to the Left in politics, pushing once more for the anti-monarchical forces of England to move forward, although this time not via a major civil war, but with the rise of the 1678 Whig Party, the "liberals" of the time, with more egalitarian ideals, and fully in favor of Parliament, and offering also a new, and more stable, long-term political plan against England's conservative forces: the Crown, the Tory Party, and the Church of England. The Whigs soon established the more egalitarian Parliament then as the ultimate power over the country, this after the anti-monarchical 1688–89 Glorious Revolution.

Half a century later the cycle repeated itself again, with yet one more "supercycle" peaking, and Europe again being hit by a massive financial downturn, one triggered by the 1720 South Sea Bubble, and which also caused a major market collapse, and the ruining scores of businesses, and a much reduced economic activity in Europe for at least a decade; in short, another depression. Even the smartest people of this time lost their entire life savings, including the physicist Isaac Newton, who, it should be noted, was no financial ignoramus, having, just a few decades earlier, ran Britain's Royal Mint. And yet, even with all his financial experience, he still lost his shirt to the South Sea Bubble burst, ruining him for the later part of his life. It shows how even extremely well-informed, intelligent people can be taken by surprise by such a "supercycle," again because "supercycles" happen only once in a life time, thus, leaving even the most informed largely unprepared for such extreme and utter ruinous consequences.

This 1720s depression also led to another *major* shift to the Left in politics. One of the most salient examples of this era came with the return of the Whig Party in Britain. The most famous political figure here was Sir Robert Walpole, Britain's first Prime Minister, and a top Whig leader that changed the entire direction of the country by negotiating sweeping peace deals, ending many expensive wars at the time. He also lowered taxes, and even reduced debts to ensure more financial stability. Taking advantage of the then rising influence of the Whig's over the House of Commons, he also pushed for a far more stable government, with the Prime Minister now fully in charge, and the only liaison between the Crown and Parliament. These reforms were also credited with creating the foundation of the stable cabinet system Britain has enjoyed to this day.

This major shift to the Left at this time also hit Colonial America, with its rise of the First Awakening, an intense religious revival period that lasted well into the 1730s and 1740s, which emphasized a more emotional religious experience, and stronger drive towards salvation and personal piety. It was also highly egalitarian, challenging predominant and more hierarchical churches of this time, the Anglican and Congregationalists. America's First Awakening also led to a democratization of religion with open-air sermons, widespread conversions, and a more personal relationship with God. It propelled new denominations, such as the Baptists and Methodists, and fueled more unity among the thirteen colonies, which historians see now as the basis for the later 1776 American Revolution, and the rise of America's independent identity.

The following depression happened, again, some 40 to 50-years later, and again the peak of another "supercycle" hitting the economy in 1772, and leading Europe once more into a major financial crash, with twenty British banking houses here now halting all payments, and with many going bankrupt and freezing the entire financial system. One source from this era commented: "No event for 50 years past has been remembered to have given so fatal a blow both to trade and public credit."[178] Notice the line here about *not remembering an event like it in 50 years*, suggesting yet again this half-a-century "supercycle" of rising and waning of the global economy. The 1772 crash also sank the American colonies into a decade-long economic depression. According to two experts, economists Peter Lindert and Jeffrey Williamson, "America's real income per capita dropped by about 22%" between 1774 and 1800, making this depression "almost as steep" as that of the 1930s, or Great Depression, "and certainly longer."[179] And in keeping with the same 40 to 50-year pattern discussed here, this 1772 depression also fueled a major shift to the Left: America's 1776 Revolution and its incredibly radical egalitarian push, one that

---

[178] *The Gentleman's Magazine and Historical Chronicle* (London: June 1772) MDCCLXXII, p. 293.

[179] *https://voxeu.org/article/america-s-revolution-economic-disaster-development-and-equality*

even radicalized America's wealthy elites into breaking away from Britain, framing America's Republic and its Constitution, and then its Bill of Rights, all very radical for the time. The British-American thinker Thomas Pain penned at this time his revolutionary pamphlet, *Common Sense*, very popular reading back then. Philadelphia sought to become the most democratic place in the world; the state of Vermont banned slavery in 1777; and New Jersey temporarily gave the women the vote — all, again, extremely egalitarian pushes, typical of what we would now call the Left. Even *after* the US became independent, its 1786 Shay's Rebellion again pushed for popular rights, forcing some US states to even allow for debt-relief for farmers, and for distributing free food for the hungry, all signs of egalitarian causes in trying economic times.[180]

Ever since, every US depression has gone on to fuel a major shift to the Left. The Depression of 1837, or America's "First Great Depression," resulted in the rise of the Whig Party, very progressive for its time. And the depression of 1873-93, or Long Depression, also resulted in the very strong rise of populists and progressive politics. And the 1930s Great Depression resulted in Roosevelt's New Deal. All these three depressions also fit well in this 50-year overall "supercycle" in the economy. As one New Deal supporter told Roosevelt back in the 1930s: "Your administration has made possible the continuance of American institutions for at least fifty years... You have brought it back to the people."[181] Notice how in this remark the same idea of a fifty years term, and almost exactly the time when Ronald Reagan would later come to the presidency and started that full turn against the Left that we still see today.

---

[180] *https://alphahistory.com/americanrevolution/economic-crisis-of-the-1780s/*

[181] Quoted in: Talbot, David. *The Devil's Chessboard. Allen Dulles, the CIA, and the Rise of America's Secret Government.* New York, NY: HarperCollins, 2019, p. 63.

All these depressions fell within this overall 40 to 50-year cycle. The only exception was the mid-1970s, when, instead of a depression, ended up in a severe and long *stagflation* that lasted about a decade. This stagflation period fell within this same 40 to 50-year "supercycle," the difference was that, since there was no depression, there was no big shift to the Left, but one even further to the Right. But this has been an exception in the last 400 years or so of history; clearly an *unprecedented* event.

This very long shift to the Right staring in the mid-1970s was due to a massive expansion of the postwar economy, or Golden Age of Capitalism, with its unprecedented 1950s and 60s expansion, likely saving us from a 1970s Great Depression, but instead giving us a decade-long stagflation. But the overall 40 to 50-year "supercycle" here still seemed unbroken, and if this was correct, it should be surmised then that we might still see again a major depression within the next 40 or 50 years, counting from the mid-1970s, or sometime around the mid-2020s or early 2030s, and with it, a new big shift to the Left. Few might forecast such a major change to the Left today. After having no depressions for almost a century, and no corresponding *big* shifts of the Left either, the Right has been to look endless, with experts now talking then of a future Neofeudal system in the future, with modern society reverting to medieval-like extreme wealth concentration, corporate supremacy over public life, and a fading middle class. Thus, forecasting a major shift to the Left today might seem crazy. But plenty of experts have been warning of such a depression hitting perhaps sometime in the mid-2020s, as one expert, Nouriel Roubini, for instance, was already guessing at.

Predictions of a depression were also being made also by the likes of the IMF, the World International Forum, and even the Federal Reserve. One top expert, Jeffrey Gundlach, for instance, suggested that this major downturn (which he didn't call a *depression*, but something much like it) might hit by the late-2020s, or even later, by the early-2030s.

The influence of a 40 to 50-year "supercycle" has been studied also by the US historians William Strauss and Neil Howe in their well-known book, *The Fourth Turning: An American Prophecy*. The only big different here was that these two authors broke down these 40 or 50-year cycles into two parts, each 20 to 25 years long, and each called a "turning." That made for a more detailed study, but one that still added to 40 to 50-year "supercycles" if we added two *turnings* together. Howe and Strauss also saw today's Very Long Shift to the Right as eventually reaching a limit, and thus ending the rightwing shift seen today, with the rich "getting richer and the poor poorer," and then swinging back to more equitable distributions, and with politics flowing in this opposite direction. This incoming major shift to the Left would go from predominantly *individualistic* ideals (as was the case today) to *collectivistic* ones; from *inequality* to more *equality*. Strauss and Howe also spoke of this major social and political shift coming about in around 2015,[182] which didn't happen, but in a prior book, *Generations*, they suggested the year 2020, far closer to the 2020s commonly suggested by others. The likely reason for this off-timing was that Strauss and Howe didn't consider geopolitics which may make shifts last longer and only measured the turnings based on the length of generations alone.[183]

But the basic question still remained, *when* would this next

---

[182] Strauss, William and Neil Howe. *The Fourth Turning: An American Prophecy—What the Cycles of History Tell Us About America's Next Rendezvous with Destiny*. New York; Broadway Books, 1998, p. 18. *http://www.fourthturning.com/*

[183] Strauss, William and Neil Howe. *Op. cit.*, pp. 108-109. According to Strauss-Howe, their cycle takes a society from collectivistic ideals to individualistic ones, and then back, in what the authors call a "fourth turning."

depression happen, and, with it, its corresponding leftwards shift? The hardest part of forecasting: *timing*. The most reliable forecasts were made by very large computer simulations, with tens of thousands data entry points, and covering the whole world economy. But such massive forecasts were also expensive, and usually available only to top 1%, and protected by very tight confidentiality agreements.[184] In this book, thus, we will have to do with publically available forecasts, and use this macro information as the only guide to guess at the timing of any such future great depression.

Publically available forecasts

Such forecasts vary enormously. Famously, economist Janet Yellen, while at the helm of the US Federal Reserve, remarked that a big recession like the one in 2008 was unlikely to happen again "in our lifetime," she said.[185] She even added here that the US was far more resilient than most might predict. The Harvard Business School also agreed, and in 2020 it stated that: "The U. S. is not headed toward a new Great Depression," at least, it said, as long as price stability continued[186] —a big *if*, which, by the way, had perhaps fallen apart with the rise of inflation in 2022, and the growing geological instability of the 2020s in general.

But other forecasts are far more pessimistic. The Nobel Prize winner for economics, Robert Shiller, for instance, once

---

184 *http://www.businessinsider.com/what-a-long-economic-winter-feels-like-2016-10*
https://www.zerohedge.com/news/2014-05-13/if-economic-cycle-theorists-are-correct-2015-2020-will-be-devastating-us
https://www.wsj.com/articles/economists-think-the-next-u-s-recession-could-begin-in-2020-1525961127
https://www.forbes.com/sites/nextavenue/2018/08/03/is-the-next-recession-on-its-way/#d313f4548376

185 *https://www.cnbc.com/2017/06/27/yellen-banks-very-much-stronger-another-financial-crisis-not-likely-in-our-lifetime.html*

186 *https://hbr.org/2020/05/the-u-s-is-not-headed-toward-a-new-great-depression*

remarked that: "A repeat of the Great Depression is now a possibility because economists, the government, and the general public have in recent years grown complacent. They have forgotten the lessons of the 1930s."[187] At least *a possibility*, he said. Also, a top hedge fund manager, and well-known Wall Street guru, Ray Dalio, has also been forecasting a such a major downturn for many years now, which, he said, "could be worse than the last one," that is, worse than the 2008 Global Financial Crisis.[188]

Another dedicated student of economic data, the British investor Jeremy Grantham, also said that today's stock market looked already much like it did during "the crash that triggered the [1930s] Great Depression," thus concluding that there was "a huge divergence" that had not been seen since the 1929 and 2000 "super bubbles," and suggesting then that a large future crash would be much more in line with the 1930s type Great Depression than with any ordinary recession.[189]

Another well-known economist, Nouriel Roubini (one of the few, by the way, that correctly predicted the 2008 housing crash), also forecasted a depression by "the middle of the coming decade" —or mid-2020s—, saying also that it would be so bad he had already dubbed it the *Greater Depression*, since it would be way *worse* than that of the 1930s.[190] the reason that modern depression could be more chaotic than in the 1930s was due to extreme interconnectedness, digital reliance, and

---

[187] Akerlof, George A., and Robert J. Shiller. *Animal Spirits. How Human Psychology Drives the Economy, and Why it Matters for Global Capitalism*. Princeton, NJ: Princeton University Press, 2009, p. vii.

[188] *https://www.barrons.com/articles/ray-dalio-financial-crisis-1536765634 1*

[189] *https://markets.businessinsider.com/news/stocks/jeremy-grantham-gmo-bubble-warning-superbubble-1929-2000-sp500-stocks-2022-*

[190] *https://nymag.com/intelligencer/2020/05/why-the-economy-is-headed-for-a-post-coronavirus-depression-nouriel-roubini.html*
https://www.theguardian.com/business/2020/apr/29/ten-reasons-why-greater-depression-for-the-2020s-is-inevitable-covid

higher debt, potentially causing then faster, sharper collapses than in the 1930s. Also, there was also vastly more debt today than in the 1930s. In nominal terms, today's national debt was more than 2,000 times higher than that seen in 1930. As a percentage, this then represented an increase of over 83,000% in the debt since 1940. And as a Percentage of GDP (what is known as the Economic Burden), the debt-to-GDP ratio had also grown to the extreme. It had gone from roughly 17% in 1930, to about 40–44% by 1934–1936, and then to roughly 112% just after World War II, but this only for a very short time, and due only to the massive cost of this war, and after which it was immediately cut back to the far lower levels seen for the next half a century or so. But today, this debt-to-GDP ratio had risen again, exceeding 120% by 2024, and continuing up.[191]

Even the International Monetary Fund, not given to panics, now issued dire warnings about a future "financial meltdown," the result, it said, of "reckless" market behavior, and speaking also of a "second Great Depression" —yes, *second Great Depression*, the exact words used by the IMF. The IMF also warned here that "capitalism is running amok," and that this impending "meltdown" might not be preventable. "Large challenges loom," the IMF added, making it, thus, very hard "to prevent" a Great Depression 2.0.[192] One top IMF director even stated that the world was ill-prepared for such a crash, pointing out that debt today was just too high —much higher than in 2008—; and that growth was far weaker than ever before, and getting even weaker.[193] The IMF also reminded us

[191] *https://www.us-debt-clock.com/blog/us-debt-clock-by-year*

[192] *https://www.theguardian.com/business/2018/oct/03/world-economy-at-risk-of-another-financial-crash-says-imf*

[193] *https://www.theguardian.com/business/2018/dec/11/imf-financial-crisis-david-lipton* Markups had risen by 8% worldwide between 2000 and 2015. Among top-tier companies these were even higher, increasing by 30% in a few decades.

that, since 2022, there was a "steady worsening" of all "G20 economies," all of which had dropped to levels "that signal[ed] contraction," and a global slowdown in both "advanced and emerging market economies." Such outlooks, the IMF said, were worse even than the 1930s Great Depression, or than the 1973-74 Oil Shock, or than the 2008 Global Financial Crisis,[194] all pointing at a bad future slump, similar even to the one proposed by Nouriel Roubini about a future *Greater Depression*.

But where was all this pessimism coming from?

Well, *from the data*. Since the mid-1970s, financial crises worldwide *tripled* in number —this between 1973 and 1997.[195] Instability and corruption have also gone up, and financial "scandals" have also tripled after 1973.[196] These years were also when the greatest deregulation and "globalization" had begun. Crises now have also only become ever more severe since the mid-1970s, as was the case, for instance, of Europe's 1992 financial crisis, or Black Wednesday, a crash so bad Great Britain had to withdraw its currency from the European Exchange Rate Mechanism completely —a system that had been put in place precisely to help maintain stability in the area. The later giant financial crisis that hit Asia in 1997 also took out entire stock markets in South Korea, Hong Kong, Philippines, Taiwan, Thailand, Indonesia, and Singapore. The

---

https://www.npr.org/sections/money/2019/04/16/713615612/a-guardian-of-global-capitalism-warns-capitalism-has-a-problem?
https://www.youtube.com/watch?v=rD7KNVzkLPw

[194] *https://www.investopedia.com/imf-warns-worsening-economy-6828582*

[195] See: Wolf, Martin. *Fixing Global Finance.* New Haven, CT: Yale University Press, 2008, p. 31.

[196] After 1973, the number of scandals worldwide jumped drastically, reaching routinely to over 1,200 scandals per year, and sometimes more than 2,000, and one time reaching 2,400 (this in 2001). See: *https://www.ineteconomics.org/perspectives/blog/how-well-does-financial-reg-work*

damage was monumental.[197] Taiwan's industrial output here fell by an astounding 30%, worse than with 1930s Great Depression in the US. Indonesia's president resigned. Thailand's Prime Minister also had to resign. And the Philippines entered half a decade of political instability. Malaysia's leader only managed to survive thanks to strict capital controls preventing a complete money hemorrhage. Almost everywhere locals in Asia blamed big US banks and corporate forces for this crash.[198]

The US was also at ever greater risk. A well-known economist, Steven Keen, pointed out that America's public debt almost doubled between 2009 and 2017, now surpassing the total GDP of the country, and growing by half a trillion dollars every year *at least* —with a less conservative estimates putting this annual growth at *one trillion*, and rising. Either way, it was growing *four or five times* faster than the underlying economy, clearly an unsustainable rate.[199] Just the interest payments for this debt were now one of the US federal government's largest single budget items.[200] Almost everyone in America was worried about it, with 96% of the public wanting this debt reduced.[201] The US was then turning into a "debt zombie," as Steven Keen also called it, only able to meet its payments by

---

197 *https://web.archive.org/web/20121004232627/ http://blogs.telegraph.co.uk/finance/thomaspascoe/100020478/britain-is-following-argentina-on-the-road-to-ruin/*

198 *https://www.thebalance.com › Investing › International Investing › Getting Started*

199 Under President Obama, the US economy had been growing at an average of only 2.1%. *https://www.usgovernmentdebt.us/debt_deficit_history*

200 Some $310 billion dollars per year in 2017. *http://www.mathmotivation.com/money/usdebt.html*
https://www.thebalance.com › Investing › US Economy › National Debt
https://www.cnbc.com/2016/12/19/interest-payments-could-become-one-of-the-federal-govts-biggest-line-items.html

201 *http://reason.com/poll/2011/05/06/public-opinion-debt*
http://www.people-press.org/2012/06/14/debt-and-deficit-a-public-opinion-dilemma/

contracting ever more debt.[202]

Aside from the unbelievable mountains of unplayable debt, the US was also facing a mountain of toxic financial "assets," or "instruments" called *derivatives,* so massive and risky that these alone could demolish the entire system. (A *derivative,* by the way, was like a "side bet," a contract made from another contract, which, by itself, added no value, but that could be priced, theoretically at least, and thus allowing it to be bought and sold, even if it value was largely fictional.) The massive size of these derivatives —evolving into ever more convoluted forms, or *complex derivatives,* making them even harder to value— has become so large that, according to the Bank for International Settlements, their total worldwide value in 2017 *on paper* was some *15 times larger* than the value of the total world economy.[203] How could *anything* possibly cover even the nominal value of all these derivatives? There just wasn't enough money in the whole wide world to cover it. A collapse here would devastate finance, and leave regulatory agencies and governments unable to cope.[204] The American financier Warren Buffet called such derivatives "weapons of financial mass destruction," which, he said, allowed for "huge amounts of speculation," and a "very dangerous" situation, making "very

---

[202] Keen, Steven. *Can We Avoid Another Financial Crisis?* New York, NY: Polity Press, 2017. These huge levels of debt would make a new financial downturn "hard to escape," *The Economist* had said, especially given how "constrained" central banks were, and how deeply divided politics remained. See: *https://www.economist.com/leaders/2018/10/11/the-next-recession*

[203] Total derivatives added up an astonishing $1.2 quadrillion dollars out of a total world GDP of $77.99 trillion dollars.
http://money.visualcapitalist.com/worlds-money-markets-one-visualization-2017/
http://statisticstimes.com/economy/countries-by-projected-gdp.php
http://www.businessinsider.com/graph-worlds-debt-share-by-country-2015-8
https://www.marketwatch.com/story/this-is-how-much-money-exists-in-the-entire-world-in-one-chart-2015-12-18
https://www.poder360.com.br/wp-content/.../2017/.../global-wealth-report-2017-en.p...

[204] *https://www.bis.org/publ/qtrpdf/r_qt1506b.htm*

large derivatives positions" "a potential time bomb."[205]

The geopolitical expert Peter Zeihan also forecasted that today's global "financial wave will crest at some point between 2020 and 2024," after which capital growth would dry up, causing a major weakening of economies. Zeihan also pointed out that 13 of the *top* 15 world economies were already (in the late 2000s) "financially distressed," including Germany, the US, and the UK. China, he said, would fare worse, likely disintegrating by the 2030s.[206] Or as *The Economist* would put it, "bit by bit" these economies were weakening, showing that growth wouldn't "last forever."[207] It's true 2024 came and went, and that such core economies didn't fall apart, but in 2025 Zeihan forecasted that, "the decade from 2025 to 2035 was the decade where that was all going to break down," with the *all going to break down* line referring precisely to a "Global Depression," as Zeihan himself put it in the title of his podcast.[208] Demographers were also issuing dire warnings. They had long found that the largest and wealthiest US generation —the Baby Boomers—, were retiring at a record pace, no longer putting money *into* the system, but getting it *out*, thus *reversing* the capital flows that for decades have fueled US growth. Since 2018, some 10,000 Baby Boomers were now leaving the workforce *every day*.[209] As Peter Zeihan

---

[205] *http://www.afr.com/markets/derivatives/warren-buffett-still-says-derivatives-are-weapons-of-mass-destruction-20150617-ghpw0a*
http://www.telegraph.co.uk/business/2016/05/01/warren-buffett-issues-a-fresh-warning-about-derivatives-timebomb/

[206] Zeihan, Peter. *The Accidental Superpower.* New York, NY: Hatchet Book Group, 2014, p. 148.

[207] *https://www.economist.com/leaders/2025/07/17/bit-by-bit-the-world-economys-resilience-is-being-worn-away*

[208] Zeihan, Peter. "Global Depression Coming Sooner than Expected," (video), in *Zeihan on Geopolitics*, Dec. 5, 2025.
https://www.youtube.com/watch?v=UBMluINRans

[209] *https://finance.yahoo.com/news/americans-retiring-increasing-pace-145837368.html*

put it: "Population growth has inverted," thus: "Consumption is done. Investment is done. Capital accruing is done."[210]

Similar conclusions were reached by economist Robert J. Gordon in his very well-researched book *The Rise and Fall of American Growth*, where future growth, he found, would see *persistent* slowdowns, at least if compared to that stronger 100-year run between 1870 and 1970, a time of "life-altering scale of innovations," as Gordon put it, and which was no longer the case today, suggesting a major downturn, and also a much more persistent one.[211]

Finally, the World Economic Forum, that gathering of the top 1% elites, also believed "systemic challenges" today have, "if anything, intensified amid proliferating indications of uncertainty, instability and fragility."[212] Convoluted words, but similar to warnings issued by the IMF, Robert Shiller, Robert J. Gordon, Nouriel Roubini, Peter Zeihan, among many others: a steep rise of risk and instability in coming years.

Even the US Federal Reserve was forecasting a big slump. Not a depression, to be fair, just a "slowdown," but one that could still have, as the Fed put it, "far reaching implications," whatever that meant.[213]

Public opinion also forecasted a depression. More than half of Americans (52%) in 2022, for instance, believed a "second Great Depression" might likely hit soon.[214] The much-respected University of Michigan Consumer Sentiment Index was also turning ever grimmer since at least 2022, with its numbers at

---

[210] *https://www.financialsense.com/blog/20008/world-about-fall-demographic-cliff-warns-peter-zeihan-and-implications-will-be-enormous*

[211] Gordon, Robert. *The rise and fall of American growth*. Princeton, NJ: Princeton University Press, 2016.

[212] *https://www.euractiv.com/section/politics/news/watch-out-for-the-next-crisis-gloomy-davos-report-tells-leaders/*

[213] *https://www.wsj.com/articles/u-s-economy-flashes-signs-its-downhill-from-here-1540656002?mod=hp_lead_pos7*

[214] *https://amac.us/are-we-on-the-road-to-americas-second-great-depression/*

their "lowest level in its 70-year history",[215] and with its 2025 numbers still running on the very low side of things.[216] Yet another survey, from the University of Chicago, also "showed pervasive economic pessimism" in 2023, expressing "dim hopes for the future," and with four out of five people polled stating the economy was "not so good or poor," and almost half feeling it would "get worse in the next year."[217]

One more expert, Bert Dohmen, a frequent contributor to *Forbes* magazine, also forecasted a dire "international crisis," followed by a "10-year depression," and "much worse than the Great Depression,"[218] similar again to Nouriel Roubini's grim forecasts. And one more financial expert, Jeffrey Gundlach, gave a narrowed-down timeline for this major downturn during a Bloomberg News interview, calling for it to hit in 2027 and 2028, a part, he said, of the overall "waves of history" (or "supercycles"?), and expecting even a full reset of the entire US social "pact," including its "split" between "property relations" and "rewards." Gundlach also spoke here of a "restructuring" of institutions, finances, and politics, quoting also the *Fourth Turning* model. In short, Gundlach was most likely referring to a *depression*, or something very much like it, even if he didn't referred to it by that specific name.[219]

---

[215] *https://www.nytimes.com/2022/04/28/business/college-workers-starbucks-amazon-unions.html*

[216] *https://www.wsj.com/economy/consumers/americans-jittery-over-inflation-university-of-michigan-survey-suggests-1476cf39?mod=hp_lead_pos1*

[217] *https://www.wsj.com/articles/most-americans-doubt-their-children-will-be-better-off-wsj-norc-poll-finds-35500ba8*

[218] Dohmen, Bert. "Take Your 'Safe Money' Out of the Banks, We're Facing Crisis Greater Than 1930s," (video). Interview with Stansberry Research, May 3rd, 2023. *https://www.youtube.com/watch?v=A4-LGeYiW8U* Another well-known forecaster, Martin Armstrong, did not speak of a depression, but did predict by mid-2024 "a very long recession," lasting perhaps for four years, and marked by stagflation, war, uncertainty, and shortages. "DATE Revealed: The Coming Recession that Will Last Till 2028," (video) in *Jason Hartman*, Feb 6, 2024. *https://www.youtube.com/watch?v=ZSLKRj-Gl18*

[219] *https://www.bloomberg.com/news/videos/2025-06-11/gundlach-on-treasuries-*

Finally, one economic research and consulting firm, ITR Economics, also forecasted an incoming depression hitting during the early 2030s.[220]

But in spite of all this doom and gloom, the US economy had *still* chugged along into the present time. How come?

One reason: the massive money inflows coming into the US, estimated to be "somewhere between $1 trillion and $2.5 trillion" yearly since 2000.[221] The world was then supporting the US economy. The problem was that the majority of all this capital was not used productively. As the financial journalist Rana Foroohar once pointed out, between 2008 and 2020, just 15% of such accumulated capital went into any *productive* investments. The rest went into the pockets of the top 10%, and used almost entirely for speculation. No wonder that, even after an injection of $6 trillion dollars of new money (or QE) by the US government during the early 2020s still led only to such anemic growth, or of hiring and consumer confidence.[222]

Only 3% of all the money loaned by banks today now went into productive investments —the rest, again, went into ever growing gambling financial markets and pure speculation.[223]

Ray Dalio even argued then that the US was *already* in a

---

gold-fed-ai-private-credit-video

[220] *https://itreconomics.com/2030s-great-depression/*

[221] Zeihan, Peter. *The End of the World is Just the Beginning: Mapping the Collapse of Globalization.* New York, NY: HarperCollings, 2022, p. 213.

[222] "The Dangers of Financialization." Oct 11, 2016 (video).
https://www.youtube.com/watch?v=vtlk7WlINPQ
https://www.fitchratings.com/research/sovereigns/global-qe-asset-purchases-to-reach-usd6-trillion-in-2020-24-04-2020
No wonder also the US could afford such low interest rates during much of the 2010s —the lowest, in fact, in 4,000 years of human history. Called Quantitative Easing, or QE for short, allowed the US to continue growing for much longer than almost anywhere else. Furthermore, big business has only accelerated this concentration of wealth by buying back their own stocks to boost even more their already massive profits. (Such buy-backs, by the way, were illegal as recently as in 1982.)

[223] Lanchester, John. "For Every Winner a Loser," in *London Review of Books*. Sept., 12, 2024, p. 3.

depression today, a "hidden depression," as he called it, remaining afloat only by a vast money-printing machine, and vast flows of foreign capital, and also by a massive speculation on AI technology —this last one reaching almost half a trillion dollars just in 2024. But this was, he said, a perilous situation. The risks were absolutely huge because this was not just an AI bubble; or just a housing bubble; or just a credit card bubble; or just a student loan bubble; or just an auto loan bubble; but all of them *combined*. It was an everything bubble; an economy kept *artificially* afloat by a monetary sugar high, but that, at some point, would surely crash. No wonder *The Economist* was already warning that, if another crisis were to hit us today, this one would be a "catastrophe,"[224] with no place for anyone to hide anymore.

Previews of this catastrophe might already be here. As *The Economist* once put it, "corners of the US economy" were already showing "disconcerting portents" of trouble, as early even as in the 2010s. Michigan and Illinois, for instance, were already struggling under massive debts, both ripe for severe downturns.[225] More examples? Two American regional banks, Silicon Valley Bank and First Federal Bank of California, completely crashed back in 2023; as did one of Switzerland's two top banks, Credit Swisse, perhaps signs all of how credit was being slowly squeezed out of the markets, becoming ever more scarce and expensive. The Press always dismissed such reversals as "isolated" events, the typical damage-control spit used to appease the public. But more than half (54%) of respondents to a vast 2024 survey of top one-percenters in the World Economic Forum's *Global Risks Report*, also reported

---

[224] *https://www.economist.com/open-future/2018/09/12/the-catastrophe-if-another-global-financial-crisis-strikes*

[225] *https://www.economist.com/united-states/2019/08/31/parts-of-america-may-already-be-facing-recession*

that the world was not looking good, and expected a medium risk of a catastrophe (yes, a *catastrophe*!) within years, and almost half (46%) believed that things would only get worse in the next decade, "turbulent" times, whatever that meant; and, finally, most believed that the most serious risk know was an economic downturn —both in the US, and in more than 20 European nations.[226]

In 2025, the well-known financial reporter Andrew Ross Sorkin published a book called: *1929: Inside the Greatest Crash in Wall Street History*, where he argued also that a depression-level economic collapse could happen again, and in the not too distant future, and warned also that today's market conditions also mirrored the excessive leverage, speculation, and overconfident mindset seen right before the 1929 crash. High levels of debt, and risks *within* private credit vehicles *outside* traditional bank supervision were similar as in 1929. Today's AI-powered markets and top chip companies were also not unlike those speculative company bubbles of the 1920s, driven by then new technologies like the radio and the automobile. Allowing ever more average investors access to ever riskier, less-regulated, private assets was also very much like the 1920s push for mass market stock participation, which, when reversed, caused the widespread devastation that fueled the later 1930s depression. Even the ignoring of today's alarm bells of overinvestment was similar to the ignoring of the same patterns back in 1929. Sorkin, a Wall Street friendly author, argued that today's political and regulatory landscape would react differently than in 1929 (being then more hopeful about things than many other authors), but even he had to admit that the intense speculative forces seen today remained very much as dangerous as back in 1929.

---

[226] *https://www.weforum.org/stories/2024/01/global-risks-report-country-comparison-economy/*

Finally, one expert investigative economist, James S. Henry, and writer for the media outlet *DC Report*, also reported on significant, often quiet, recent spikes in Federal Reserve money injections to big banks, or repo market. Henry here interpreted these injections as signals of banks suddenly being very short on cash, which could mean a sign of a future financial crisis, perhaps not too far into the future. The Federal Reserve Bank of New York, or NYFed, had begun injecting, *silently*, tens of billions of dollars into banks in around late 2025. This NYFed also provided $17 billion in cash to an unknown bank or banks on the morning after Christmas 2025, and another $34 billion shortly after that, this following a removal of caps on emergency lending. Henry then argued that such actions indicated that at least one "Too Big to Fail" bank had faced a serious cash shortage, much like in the shortage buildup to the 2008 financial crisis. Finally, America's repurchase market — where financial institutions borrowed from each other— was also opaque and remained a hidden source of systemic risk, hiding the growing dangers faced by today's financial system, which could be much larger than even imagined by most authors.

Can a government stop an economic crisis?

What if there is a major economic downturn? What could be done to reverse it? Contrary to popular belief, after a crash, governments can't stop such downturns. Many might think presidents can direct economies, and they even blame them for recessions and/or depressions. But that's just scapegoating. History suggests the *economy* is the one that controls the *policy*, not the other way around.[227]

[227] *https://www.wsj.com/articles/ SB10001424052702304024604575173632046893848 https://www.linkedin.com/pulse/why-do-debt-crises-come-cycles-ray-dalio/*

Take the 1930s Great Depression. Some thought it was started by government policies, in this case by excessive protectionism. But this has been widely discredited. Even one steadfast expert defender of "free markets," William Bernstein, has admitted that "most economic historians now believe that only a minuscule part of the huge loss of both GDP and the United States' [during the 1930s Great Depression] can be blamed on the tariff wars."[228]

This was something that even the staunchest defenders of "free markets" had to contend with: that once an economy goes on freefall, there was little a government could do to improve things. Even the very pro-"free market" US President Herbert Hoover had to give up on his long-held belief in *laissez faire*, or "free markets" during the calamitous 1930s depression. Even a huge fiscal conservative, Hoover still had to increase public spending at least enough to feed the hungry. He hated it. But people were desperate, unemployed, broke, and frantic. So he had to help, and had to start spending government money to help. Again, policy here *followed* reality, not the other way around.

Some credited the next president, Roosevelt, for "saving" America from the Great Depression, and doing so with his New Deal. But Roosevelt's New Deal didn't get us *out* of the Great Depression. It only got us *through* it. His New Deal fed the poor, yes; it protected workers, and even the middle classes. It was good for people; again, yes. But the New Deal didn't *end* the depression: it just made it more survivable; preventing it from more widespread popular uprisings that might endanger the privileges of elites. It never fully *controlled* the economy. The depression kept on going for the whole of the 1930s in spite of Roosevelt's spending, and it would then last a total of 12 years,

---

[228] Bernstein, William J. *A Splendid Exchange. How Trade Shaped the World.* New York, NY: Atlantic Monthly Press, 2008, p. 354.

ending only after the US entered World War II in 1941, and when it began an absolutely massive injection of new money to pay for its military buildup against Germany and Japan. Only then did its economy fully recovered, and only then did the Great Depression definitely end.

Policies also do not necessarily determine economic growth, as the expert economic historian Paul Barioch has also found. Using 200 years of data, he found that neither "free trade," nor protectionism were all that effective at igniting an economy. "Free trade" was actually the worst for stimulating growth. There was no evidence in the data that such a policy had *ever* accelerated *anything* economic in the last 200 years. In fact, this policy had almost always done the opposite, lowering growth rates every time it was used. After examining these 200 years of data, Barioch also concluded that economies generally followed their *own* cycles, for the most part independent from government policies. [229]

The Nobel Prize-winning economists Abhijit Banerjee and Esther Duflo also found that "free market" policies didn't help much, in particular that favored today of giving tax breaks to the rich.[230]

Of course politicians keep promising magical fixes. But as Abhijit Banerjee and Esther Duflo also suggested, the best policy seemed to be a *pragmatic* approach,[231] precisely what

---

[229] Interestingly, protectionist policies had a stronger correlation with growth. But the real forces behind growth are international and geographical advantages. See: Barioch, Paul. *Economics and World History. Myths and Paradoxes*. Chicago: Chicago University Press, 1993.
www.larouchepub.com/.../eirv23n36-19960906_016-free_trade_is_an_aberration_no...

[230] Banerjee, Abhijit, and Esther Duflo. *Good Economics for Hard Times*. New York, NY: PublicAffairs, 2019, p. 174-175. No wonder economists were so distrusted. "Only politicians ranked lower," one poll found; with 25% of the public distrusting economists. Even economists themselves don't trust "their own field of expertise." Banerjee, *op. cit.*, p. 4.

[231] Abhijit Banerjee and Esther Duflo also suggest, again, in their 2011 book *Poor Economics: A Radical Rethinking of the Way to Fight Global Poverty*, suggested more

Roosevelt's New Deal had done: free cheese for the hungry. And it worked. But, again, it only by getting us *through* the depression, not necessarily getting us *out of it*, or *solving* the economy.

So, what if a new Great Depression were to hit us today? Would a "new" New Deal do the trick? Perhaps. Just like Trump may be called a *Jackson on steroids*, after this Very Long Shift to the Right is ended by a future great depression, there might presumably a very strong swing back to the Left, which might even lead to some sort of *FDR on steroids*.

But today we have the added problem that current governments were already so deeply in debt that it was hard to imagine how much more could they spend to get us through a new depression, and one also much bigger than that of the 1930s.[232]

And alternative to spending might be debt forgiveness. As President Thomas Jefferson wrote in 1813: "the perpetuation of debt has drenched the earth with blood and crushed its inhabitants under burdens ever accumulating."[233]

Both the private and public debts today were already completely out of control, and debt was also then the most evident problem facing today's economy. Debt forgiveness in history has also had some great successes. Right after Independence, deeply in debt farmers got some limited degree of forgiveness in some states, especially after the 1786 Shay's

---

growth did not necessarily even help alleviate poverty. They suggested that rising the quality —not necessarily the quantity— of life was the more effective way to help the people. Banerjee, *op. cit.*, p. 19.

[232] Back in 1930 the US still worked with a surplus of $734 million dollars. See: *Proposed Constitutional Amendments to Balance the Federal Budget, Volume 1: A Legislative History.* Washington, DC: U.S. Government Printing Office, 1994, p. 21. *https://www.theguardian.com/books/2018/aug/12/crashed-adam-tooze-decade-of-financal-crisis-review*
http://ic.galegroup.com/ic/whic/ReferenceDetailsPage/ReferenceDetailsWindow

[233] *http://www.let.rug.nl/usa/presidents/thomas-jefferson/letters-of-thomas-jefferson/jefl219.php*

Rebellion, which forced the then brand new US government to place moratoriums on some of these farmer's debts, and even cut their taxes to alleviate their troubling plights.

More recently, Soviet Russia also once recanted all its debts with foreign lenders in 1917, turning itself into a world pariah, but also fueling the hugely rapid 1930s Soviet industrialization, which would defeat the Germans, and, after World War II, also lead this nation to the status of a global superpower. This growth didn't last forever, but it sure gave the Soviets a good spring that lasted for almost half a century.

Also Germany and Japan after World War II had both their debts forgiven by the victorious allies, leading to extraordinary the economic revivals during the postwar era: the much admired German and Japanese post-war economic "miracles."

But debt forgiveness was still a rarity in history. The ultra-rich hate it. It was, after all, what kept the ultra-rich, ultra-rich. You took that away, and they would probably cease to exist. Thus, outside of revolutions, extreme catastrophes, or real bad military defeats, debt forgiveness was a rarity in history. The ultra-rich rarely, if ever, allowed for it. The last *widespread* debt forgiveness in Western history to help the common people, for example, was perhaps that of *ancient Greece*, some 2,400 years ago! It had great results, leading to the much admired Greek miracle of that classical era, one that still is the main inspiration of all Western societies for almost every field, science, philosophy, art and literature. It surged after the radical democratic revolutions of the time, and their exceptional success at *removing* the ultra-rich from power, in some cases, for centuries, like in the ancient city-state of Argos. But again, such a policy of debt forgiveness was an exception. And such policies reversed later by the Persian victories over the Greeks, which then led to inequality to return with the reinstatement of the predatory debt systems, systems that reign supreme to this very day.

In ancient Rome the commoners also tried to push for debt forgiveness. But the ultra-rich of this time made sure it didn't happen. For 100 years, these ultra-rich led a brutal war against anyone that tried to forgive any debts. These ultra-rich Roman Senators, for instance, even ordered the killing of peaceful and lawful reformers when they asked for some land redistribution. The Senators here then unleashed a series of assassinations of the reforming Gracchi brothers that started in 133 BCE. The first of these Gracchi brothers was killed, and the thugs of the ultra-rich then kill 300 of his followers. Ten years later, a new cadre of thugs tried to kill the second brother. They didn't succeed, but they did force him to commit suicide rather than surrender to the brutality of these goons. After that, another 300 supporters of this brother were also executed. Romans rebelled yet again somewhat later. But an influential general, Sulla, in an unprecedented act, turned the Roman Army on Rome itself, and managed to put down this new uprising, too. Sulla later put down one more uprising, and also by yet again marching the Army on the city, this time proclaiming himself dictator and going on killing spree after anyone who had opposed him previously. The Roman historian Plutarch said of this time: "Sulla now began to make blood flow, and he filled the city with deaths without number or limit."[234] Finally, Julius Cesar also tried one last time to forgive some debts.[235] But his changes were extremely limited. But even such mild reforms were rejected by the Senate, and this time they didn't even bother hiring any thugs to kill him: they

---

[234] *https://cof.quantumfuturegroup.org/events/1310*

[235] *https://www.worldhistory.org/article/112/caesar-as-dictator-his-impact-on-the-city-of-rome/* "Caesar ordered that property must be accepted for repayment at its pre-war value. He also reinstated a previous law which forbade the holding of more than 60,000 sesterces in cash by any one person. Caesar later cancelled all interest payments due since the beginning of 49 BC and permitted tenants to pay no rent for one year."

personally stabbed him 23 times, leaving him to bleed to death on the floor of the Curia de Pompey.

Understandably, debt forgiveness has not been attempted all that much since Roman times. The reason was clear: anyone who tried to forgive debts would almost always be killed.

Just ask Julius Cesar.

Today, even the laws have been rewritten to make debt *eternal.* This has happened almost everywhere in the world. As the American economist Michael Hudson has pointed out, debt might "polarize and enervate economies," but it still was the way forward almost everywhere.[236] *Debt never dies.* In a future depression, thus, leaders might try a less risky approach. They might, for instance, resort to devaluating currencies. They've done this before, during the 1930s, for instance, when Franklin Delano Roosevelt confiscated all privately held gold in 1933, and then decreed that any gold above $100 dollars in value had to be handed over to the US Federal Reserve, the Feds then paid for $20.67 per ounce of gold, and then the very next year, it then increased the price of gold to $35, giving the Federal Reserve a neat 69% profit.[237] This was, incidentally, how Roosevelt paid for a good part of his New Deal.

Nixon did something similar in 1971. When facing an accelerating stagflation since the late 1960s, he took the US Dollar off the gold standard, turning it into a fiat currency. Since then, its value has turned into pure fiction, *In God We Trust,* indeed.

And a new devaluation might be on its way today. After all, money these days was already being turned into mere digital accounts that only exist electronically, with nothing to back it

---

236 Hudson, Michael. *Killing the Host. How Financial Parasites and Debt Destroy the Global Economy.* Dresden, Germany: Islet-Verlag, 2015, pp. 9-11.

237 *https://www.history.com/this-day-in-history/fdr-takes-united-states-off-gold-standard*

up other than the numbers on servers. Did money *even exist anymore*?

During the 2000s the government's Quantitative Easing led to yet one more massive distortion of the value of money. Interest rates then fell to almost 0%, even going negative in some parts, something unprecedented in all of human history. When had interest rates ever gone negative ever before? And what did that mean for the value of money? Again, this is an unprecedented world, and a future devaluation to deal with a future depression might not take the form of any previous devaluations, but of something even more radical, perhaps like the "bail-ins" seen during the 2010s in some parts of the world.

In a "bail-in" depositors simply have all their money taken away from them by locking them out of their bank accounts, as happened in Cyprus and Greece in 2015, and later also in Lebanon. It was the destruction of money at a whole new level, dispossessing the public of their entire life savings. This might be the only solution left for the future: destroy all the money, destroy all savers; wipeout all value, especially for anyone in the bottom 90%. It might be Machiavellian, downright evil, but what other way was there to cope with another depression? One might personally buy gold and hunker down somewhere, but this, of course, was not a full solution, just an individual palliative. A broader solution would have to come from politics, from effectively limiting the economic power of the elites, and their ability to fleece the treasury. But for this to happen, a much larger and further push would be needed politically towards a stronger democracy, even perhaps a direct type of democracy like that of Ancient Athens, for instance, where the people held *all* the power, and not only through elected representatives, but *directly*, via assemblies: the only place where government decisions could be made, and only via a majority vote, and only place them could then decide economic policy, and direct the direction of the nation. Could this be possible in the near future? It might, especially if we take a look at the way politics is shaping up today, ever more radical, and ever more intense and even violent, and ever more class-based, it seems. These are the politics of the future, and the subject of the following chapter.

5. THE POLITICS OF THE FUTURE

A *full third* of Americans today felt the "urge to protest," as a 2018 Gallup poll found, eclipsing even the tumultuous 1960s, when this same "urge" was just 10%.[238] By these numbers, today's public was three times more rebellious than even in the 1960s. Many Americans also now even doubted that the "US system" could fix the country's "long term problems" anymore, with most Democrats believing also that a proper solution today would involve "overhauling" the entire nation.[239]

The urge to protest among American women seemed

---

[238] Women here were leading the charge, with 43% feeling the need to protest in 2018, against only 28% among men. The top issue were women's rights, followed by immigration and gun control. A leftwards shift was also present here, with 60% of "liberals" feeling the "urge to protest," against only 21% among "conservatives." *https://news.gallup.com/poll/241634/one-three-americans-felt-urge-protest.aspx* The British newspaper The Guardian, reported that protests in the US had now risen as "high as the roaring 60s." *https://www.theguardian.com/world/2019/oct/25/protests-rage-around-the-world-hong-kong-lebanon-chile-catalonia-iraq*

[239] *https://www.wsj.com/articles/americans-arent-sure-u-s-system-can-fix-long-term-problems-poll-finds-11561111321?mod=hp_lista_pos2*

especially high. Since 2018, women were almost twice as likely to feel the need to protest as men, with the top issues here being women's rights, followed by immigration rights, and then gun control.[240]

The 2018 "March for Our Lives," perhaps the first mass mobilization of Millennials, and seeking more gun control, was huge, spreading to some 800 towns and cities across the US, and mobilizing hundreds of thousands of younger folk on to the streets.[241]

In 2019, a mass shooting occurred at a Cielo Vista Walmart in El Paso, Texas, where a gunman killed 23 people and injured 22 others. The attack has been recognized as the deadliest act of violence targeting Hispanics in modern US history. Before the shooting, this gunman posted a racist manifesto titled "The Inconvenient Truth," citing a "Hispanic invasion of Texas" and the "Great Replacement" conspiracy theory as his inspiration.

In 2020, the Black Lives Matter protests (unleashed after the killing of a 46-year-old a Black man, George Floyd, while in custody by the Minneapolis PD) spread to not just in metropolitan areas, but even to "small towns with deeply conservative politics," places with fewer than 20,000 residents. These protests were so strong they seemed like a throwback to the 1950s and 1960s, but different in that they came not only from cities and college campuses, but even from small, white, conservative towns, like Coeur d'Alene, say, in Idaho.[242] It showed "just how widespread and fast-moving the movement is," as *The Wall Street Journal* noted.[243] Polls also showed the

---

[240] *https://news.gallup.com/poll/241634/one-three-americans-felt-urge-protest.aspx*

[241] *https://www.nationalreview.com/news/only-12-percent-of-first-time-protesters-at-march-for-our-lives-were-there-for-gun-control/*

[242] *https://www.washingtonpost.com/politics/2020/06/06/floyd-protests-are-broadest-us-history-are-spreading-white-small-town-america/*

[243] *https://www.wsj.com/articles/black-lives-matter-protests-spread-quickly-to-white-rural-areas-11592818201*

public here being "more troubled" by the killing of George Floyd than by the sporadic violence and looting. Finally, among *average* Americans, there was now an incredible 2-to-1 margin support *in favor* of the protesters, according to one poll in *The Wall Street Journal.*[244]

But what really stood out today was how most protesters now seemed more willing to contest authority, and reject long-held certainties, and even resort to open rebellion. The attack on the Capitol Building on January 6, 2021, might be one example, with far-right protesters here leaving more than 140 law enforcement officers injured, and four people dead.[245]

Individual politically-motivated attacks were also on the rise, with the far-right attack, for instance, on the husband of former Democrat House Speaker Nancy Pelosi in 2022, for instance, resulting in him being assaulted in his home by a lone assailant with a hammer, leaving his skull fractured.[246]

Two years later, another lone attacker, this one likely from the Left, shot and killed the CEO of UnitedHealthcare as a way to denounce the country's rampant healthcare abuse. The most surprising part here was the support this attacker got. One in three Americans under age 45 supported him, while only by one in five of any age supported the victim.[247] It showed an increasingly vitriolic divisiveness in the country, with one part no longer willing to even tolerate the other.

According to 2024 Gallup data, most adults (80%) now felt the country was greatly divided on its most important values, representing a record-high perceived polarization, with most

---

[244] *https://www.wsj.com/articles/americans-are-more-troubled-by-police-actions-in-killing-of-george-floyd-than-by-violence-at-protests-poll-finds-11591534801*

[245] *https://www.cnn.com/2021/01/16/politics/insurrection-investigation-washington-lockdown/index.html*

[246] *https://www.nbcnews.com/news/us-news/david-depape-man-attacked-paul-pelosi-hammer-sentenced-30-years-prison-rcna152614*

[247] *https://www.thestate.com/news/nation-world/national/article297069729.html*

seeing the nation more divided than united, and with another large majority saying the country was "spiraling out of control."[248]

A 2025 *Washington Post* poll also found that a full third of Americans now felt that *violence against the government* was sometimes *justified.*[249] One sign of this intensity came with the booing and jeering elected officials in town meetings in 2025 after President Trump allowed one non-elected, *unaccountable* entity to access to the Treasury Department and Social Security Administration databases.[250] As a result, some town meetings had to be cancelled, and done online.[251]

In 2025 a rightwing man, disguised as a police officer, killed a state representative in the State of Minnesota and her husband, and then went on to shoot and wound a state senator and his wife, all of them liberal figures. Minnesota governor Tim Walz called such attacks "targeted political violence."[252]

Also in 2015, a lone gunman shot and killed the far-right activist Charlie Kirk at the Utah Valley University, an act that President Trump immediately blamed on the 'radical left,' and insisting that, he said, "The radicals on the left are the problem, and they're vicious and they're horrible, and they're politically

---

[248] *https://www.wsj.com/articles/americans-are-more-troubled-by-police-actions-in-killing-of-george-floyd-than-by-violence-at-protests-poll-finds-11591534801 A 2020 Pew Research Institute poll found that almost all Americans (90%) now thought the two main parties were having "very strong conflicts," while just eight years earlier this percentage had been less than half of that. https://www.latimes.com/politics/newsletter/2021-10-15/us-most-divided-nation-in-worldwide-survey-essential-politics*

[249] *https://www.theguardian.com/us-news/2022/jan/02/one-three-americans-violence-government-justified-poll*

[250] *https://www.axios.com/2025/02/05/musk-doge-treasury-payments-access-read-only*

[251] *https://www.nbcnews.com/politics/congress/republican-congressman-faces-extended-boos-jeers-rowdy-town-hall-rcna196413*

[252] *https://abcnews.go.com/US/2-minnesota-lawmakers-shot-targeted-incident-officials/story?id=122840751*

savvy."[253] Some in the Left blamed Kirk's own divisive speeches for his killing, but then some such high-profile media personalities and journalists faced immediate consequences. A Reuters investigation, for instance, found that over 600 people were fired or punished for their reactions to Kirk's death.

That same year, at the Capital Jewish Museum in Washington DC, two staffers from the Israeli embassy were shot and killed in a possible rightwing attack.

That same year, a gunman with reportedly anti-vaccine views fired about 180 rounds into the CDC headquarters in Atlanta, Georgia, killing one police officer.

That same year, a sniper, likely motivated by leftwing ideals, shot three at an ICE facility in Dallas, Texas, killing one. The Homeland Security Secretary immediately stated that: "This vile attack was motivated by hatred for ICE… This shooting must serve as a wake-up call to the far-left that their rhetoric about ICE has consequences."[254]

No surprise that one news outlet characterized 2025 as "the year of political violence," as attacks like these have become more frequent, brazen, and even normalized.[255]

In 2026, one of Trump's immigration crackdowns on illegal immigrants, one aimed at Minneapolis, Minnesota, deployed thousands of agents to this city, causing local outrage, and sustained protests, with ICE officers here later shooting and killing a 37-year-old US citizen and mother of three, Renee Nicole Good. The Department of Homeland Security characterized the incident as a "domestic terror attack," which sprung open the vitriolic divide here again, and claiming Good had tried to "weaponize her vehicle" against an officer. But by

---

[253] *https://www.cnn.com/2025/09/13/politics/trump-rhetoric-democrats-charlie-kirk*

[254] *https://www.dhs.gov/news/2025/09/24/dhs-issues-statement-targeted-attack-dallas-ice-facility*

[255] *https://nolabels.org/the-latest/the-year-of-political-violence/*

bystander videos showed the agent here shooting into the vehicle while standing *in front of it*, and then again *from the side* as it moved forward into traffic. Just days later, a 37-year-old US citizen and ICU nurse, Alex Pretti, was also fatally shot by a Border Patrol agent during an anti-ICE protest. Again, the federal account was quick, saying that agents fired here in self-defense because Pretti was armed and resisted disarming, even though witness accounts and video evidence indicated Pretti was holding a phone, not a weapon, and was being restrained and beaten *before* being shot. These killings triggered a huge statewide "ICE Out" protest and strike, with hundreds of businesses closing in solidarity, and forcing the federal government to withdraw its ICE agents. Democrats also shut down the funding for Homeland Security in Congress.

If there seemed to be one likely forecast for the immediate future in politics, this would be a continuation, and even increase of the vitriol and brutality around many of the issues that affect society today. And in this respect, the US was not alone. Such extreme protesting was also seen around the world, suggesting even a global trend here.

Similarly, today's urge to protest reached new levels in France, too, with its *Yellow Vests* protests in 2018 and 2019, when hundreds of thousands of people took to the streets of France almost without warning. The trigger here was a tax hike, including one particularly unpopular onc to fuel prices. What was new here was that protesters came from *outside* the traditional channels for protesting in France, from the Unions or political parties, and were thus seen as "self-directed."[256]

---

[256] *https://www.nytimes.com/2018/12/04/world/europe/france-economy-protests.html* Another parallel between the present time with history, was the 1830s decade of global unrest, dominated back then by the liberal Revolutions of 1830 across Europe and significant social, labor, and racial violence elsewhere. Key events included the July Revolution in France, the successful Belgian Revolution, the suppressed Polish uprising, rural "Swing" riots in Britain, and anti-abolitionist riots

The Associated Press soon called it a "full-on revolution," since protesters here even tried to burn down France's central bank. "At its height," the Associated Press also reported, "a quarter of a million people marched around France." Supported by more than 80% of the French, the demands here were radical, class-based, including "social justice," and "higher taxes on the rich, [and] more public spending to help the working class," and a "mass nationalization of French corporations."[257] As one Yellow Vest protester, a healthcare worker, put it: "We haven't had a pay rise in ten years, it's just disgusting. We're not even scraping by, it's just not possible anymore."[258] Protesters gained a million signatures, and reached, at one point, 300,000 active followers. As one protester explained: "We should have entrepreneurs, shopkeepers and artisans running this country." He felt that, "Our leaders are completely detached from reality." The goal, thus, was "to make it easier for the public to mount national referendums,"[259] a principle also known as the *right to direct initiative*, or right to remove any politician *at any time* by popular choosing. "With the internet," another protester said, "we don't need members of parliament anymore." In other words, these protests were "anti-establishment,"[260] and pursuing *direct democracy*, or the placing representatives into a place where they only had two choices: do the people's bidding, or hit the road.[261] In short,

---

in the US. Both the 1830s and the 2010s-20s reactions to the shift to the Right seemed to be global in nature.

[257] *https://apnews.com/article/84b32c4da6a14d2e9c56e3d90a0ec1ed*

[258] *https://www.thelocal.fr/20181210/frances-yellow-vests-a-movement-of-many-shades*

[259] *https://apnews.com/article/84b32c4da6a14d2e9c56e3d90a0ec1ed*

[260] *https://www.thelocal.fr/20181210/frances-yellow-vests-a-movement-of-many-shades*

[261] Chicago's Northeastern University found that blockchain voting could make voting via "a smartphone, laptop or any device with a browser and a front facing camera," and "an internet connection," and into a public ledger, running on many computer nodes, and, thus, could never be stored in one single place, or be

this was what might be a new trend in politics, *fast and furious*, one that may define, in fact, the politics of the future.

French authorities only knew to respond with savagery, attacking and injuring some 4,000 Yellow Vests in a major crackdown.[262]

It's important to note also that these protesters were not just calling for the ousting of one particular leader or ruling party, but for a complete overhaul of the entire political system and political class of the country. This was a pattern also seen all around: in Gaza, Holland, Bolivia, Egypt, Malta, Kazakhstan, Moscow, Ecuador, Hong Kong, Catalonia, Albania, and Haiti; all also linked to cost of living and deep dissatisfaction with corrupt politics. In Ecuador, the rioting here got so fierce, and so out of hand in 2019 that the country's president had to flee the capital to avoid capture, another sign of how radical and intense this unrest was now becoming.

In Chile, protesters followed this same *fast-and-furious* style. Here, a million people took to the streets to protest the bad economy, rising inequality, and a deeply unpopular metro fare hike. One demonstrator explained: "The basic salary of a nursing technician who has studied for two and half years is about 176,000 pesos (just over $250) a month. Not even a minimum wage, that's the truth."[263] Just as in France, the protests were highly insurrectional, and, also like in France, authorities responded with brutality, leaving 19 people dead,

---

influenced by any one party or special interest. It was secure and verifiable. "The cost of building [this] system is substantially less as compared to the cost of running a ballot based system," since the voter "could go to a public... library or a school... to vote." Northwestern University also found that it could be done "without sacrificing privacy for voters." It would also give users "a confirmation of their vote," something not found in paper ballots today.
https://www.economist.com/sites/default/files/northeastern.pdf

262 *https://www.thelocal.fr/20181210/frances-yellow-vests-a-movement-of-many-shades*

263 *https://www.businessinsider.com/a-look-at-what-protesters-in-chile-have-to-say-2019-10#natalia-torres-24-medical-student-5*

and 2,500 injured. They also arrested 2,800 protesters.

Iran also saw very radical protests that year, also triggered by fuel prices. It quickly spread to 21 different cities, with demonstrators here destroying a total of 731 banks, nine Islamic religious centers, and even attacking *50 military bases*! A stunning example of this kind of *fast-and-furious* protesting. But the crackdown here was also particularly extreme, with Iran's authorities leaving 1,500 protesters dead, and an untold number of arrested.

Indonesia this year also saw huge protests, also triggered by a rise in the cost of living. Thousands again took to the streets, and, again, authorities cracked down very heavily, leaving five dead and 250 injured. Some 40 police officers were also injured.

In Lebanon the 2019 protesters forced the resignation of the prime minister, and the same thing happened in Iraq, showing how they, in some cases, could take down entire administrations in a short time.

The Press soon dubbed such worldwide strife the *Global Protests of 2019.*

These protests felt like "a social revolution," according to the newspaper *The Guardian*, with a "growing demand for participatory democracy."[264] Most were calling for the replacement of the entire political class, something not seen perhaps since World War II, and yet one more sign of how radical politics were becoming this time. Given the economic despair, the inequality, everywhere on the rise, it would be reasonable also to assume that this fast-and-furious type of unrest might even become the main drive for the politics in the future, perhaps even all around the world. And authorities were already having a growing problem of *governability*; a

---

[264] *https://www.theguardian.com/world/2019/oct/25/protests-rage-around-the-world-hong-kong-lebanon-chile-catalonia-iraq*

problem with dealing with these new political demands, and even maintaining just basic overall internal order.[265] The US government, one study found, has lost almost 30% of its ability to respond to such demands, and to maintain order just between the 2010s and the mid-2020s.[266] Another study went as far as to argue that *power itself* was now melting away, including that of the military, religious institutions, and giant corporations, not just of the government. The study even argued the world was now entering an unprecedented era of instability and uncertainty.[267]

The youth played an especially active role in these *fast-and-furious* protests. They had their hopes dashed the most. As one Iraqi protesting student put it: "I studied and graduated at the top of my class from school, but no university will accept me. And even if you graduate from university there are no jobs. My friend Hussein, he graduated with a degree in English translation and he can't get a job."[268]

Much opposition here was also happening with voter's feet. Countries like Greece, Latvia, and Syria, for instance, had

---

[265] *ec.europa.eu/governance/docs/doc5_fr.pdf*
https://link.springer.com/chapter/10.1007/978-94-007-6107-0_2
http://sk.sagepub.com/reference/governance/n219.xml

[266] This data comes from the State Fragile Index and its yearly scores on the vulnerability of countries to conflict and collapse.
https://fragilestatesindex.org/comparative-analysis/
This trend is also a worldwide trend, getting only gotten worse after the full Russian invasion of Ukraine in 2022, with the world's average score "skyrocketing" from a somewhat workable 68.6, to an absolutely exploding 95.9, not too far from the highest point possible on this scale, which is 120. *https://fragilestatesindex.org/wp-content/uploads/2023/06/FSI-2023-Report final.pdf* One study even said that "nation-states" might be becoming "an increasingly nostalgic fiction."
https://assets.cambridge.org/97805218/15215/sample/9780521815215ws.pdf

[267] Naim, Moises. *The End of Power. From Boardrooms to Battlefields to Churches to States, Why Being in Charge Isn't What it Used to Be.* New York, NY: Basic Books, 2013.
https://research.stlouisfed.org/publications/economic-synopses/2016/04/29/taking-stock-income-inequality-and-the-stock-market/

[268] *https://abcnews.go.com/International/words-iraqi-protesters-speak/story?id=67071118*

already seen unprecedented numbers leave these countries, in many cases about 20% of their total populations. Venezuela was an exceptionally bad case, seeing a mind-boggling exodus of 5 million people —or 18% of its total population— and in just two years. Entire populations were clearly willing to uproot themselves, and go on the move. Even middle classes were packing up and moving this time. In 2020, US authorities notice ever-rising numbers of South American middle classes applying for asylum, and these coming not just from imploding countries like Venezuela, but from much more stable ones like Brazil.[269]

Worker strikes were also becoming astonishingly massive. In 2020, in India, for instance, 250 million workers went on strike, the largest strike in human history; and one more sign of the deep undercurrent of discontent. *One in four* of people between 15 and 64 years-old in India had gone on this strike: a quarter of this total population, something likely never before seen in modern history.[270]

Such *fast-and-furious* protests, strikes, and migrations also seemed closely linked with imploding economies. Sri Lanka was a good example. Energy-poor, and with the Russo-Ukrainian War shooting up prices for fuel, fertilizers, and food, Sri Lanka was no longer able to pay its bills, or cover the interests for its $50 billion dollar foreign debt. The country simply ran out of money, and then went into free-fall. Inflation shot up to 55%; fuel disappeared from gas stations; fishing boats remained at harbors; power outages stretched on for hours; medicine went scarce; schools closed; even government offices. Transport became very difficult. In May of 2022 the country defaulted on its debts. Garment factories, its main

---

[269] *https://www.wsj.com/articles/middle-class-migrants-fly-to-mexico-and-then-cross-u-s-border-illegally-11634117401*
[270] *https://www.workers.org/2020/01/45470/*

source of exports, also began to close. One worker put it like this: "I shiver in fear. What will I do with my life? Where will I live or work?" With tears in his eyes, another worker pleaded: "I have children —they have no food or future. We have started to eat only two meals a day." Another worker said: "Many cannot even buy sanitary pads anymore. We use cloth instead, and this has led to infections." Anyone with saleable skills was trying to emigrate. Passport lines became unprecedented. This was about the time when protesters exploded taking the streets. Led by youth and students, this unrest lasted for more than 100 days. By July protesters broke through police lines, and invaded the homes and offices of Sri Lanka's President and Prime Minister. The two then fled, and resigned.[271] Protesters wanted a total overhaul of the politics of country, "a new constitution," one said, one "that endorses people's sovereignty... through a referendum," not unlike the calls for a direct democracy of France's Yellow Vests. Sri Lanka's protesters also wanted the "president's executive powers... reduced and democratic institutions strengthened." As one leader put it: "We see this as the genuine freedom struggle of Sri Lanka because for the first time in post-independent Sri Lanka, every segment of the society —all the people— were united. The supreme power of people has overcome the power of an oppressive regime."[272] Again, no longer just ousting one administration, but of thc whole government, the same pattern as in other parts, with so many protesters going of *outside* of usual political channels, and calling for deep political change.

The irony with Sri Lanka was that just a decade or so before this country had been a poster boy of a global "free market

---

[271] *https://foreignpolicy.com/2022/07/18/sri-lanka-economic-fuel-crisis-mass-protests-wickremesinghe-rajapaksa-politics/*

[272] *https://www.aljazeera.com/news/2022/7/18/supreme-power-of-people-sri-lanka-marks-100-days-of-protests*

economic miracle."[273] Not anymore. This time it was a clear warning of the consequences of such "free market" policies, and the deep unrest they are now unleashing.

The economy almost everywhere was only getting worse. Of course, the cases of Haiti, Sudan, Venezuela, Yemen, Syria, Afghanistan, and Lebanon had already imploded; and the economies of South Sudan, the Central African Republic, the Democratic Republic of the Congo, Somalia, Libya, Argentina, and Mali, were extremely fragile, to put it mildly. Cuba, North Korea, Iran, Syria, Zimbabwe, and Venezuela were all falling apart under the weight of brutal US blockades. Pakistan's economy was also seemingly at the edge of a full-blown collapse. The economies of Cyprus, Sri Lanka, Bangladesh, Peru, Ghana, and Zambia, none of them war-torn or under blockade, were still tail-spinning from too much foreign debt and weakness.[274] Morgan Stanley identified larger economies like those of Indonesia, South Africa, Brazil, Turkey, and India as the "Fragile Five," all due to their unsustainable reliance on foreign investment and deficits. Russia, which was also hit by severe Western blockades, might also find itself at the edge of a seriously broken economy. While avoiding total collapse via capital controls and energy re-routing, Russia still faced shrinking money reserves, and declining oil revenues, leaving it in a precarious state of stagflationary pressure. And then there was China, the world's premier manufacturing hub, and yet also showing clear signs of *deflation* since the early 2020s, which might, by the way, be a sign of a future depression. China in 2023 also posted its lowest rate of economic growth in 26

---

[273] *https://www.heritage.org/international-economies/report/now-sri-lankan-free-market-economic-miracle*

[274] *https://www.reuters.com/markets/europe/turkey-caught-spiral-lira-crises-2022-06-10/*

years, with its exports here hitting a 50, or even 70-year low.[275] And if China were to fall, what other ones would follow? China kept raw materials prices up and manufacturing prices low. It held much of the world together economically. And yet it was facing many long-term troubles: a major property sector slump; weak consumer demand; massive levels of debt; and a shrinking and aging population. Southern Europe also had economies that continued to grapple with high public debt and unemployment, especially among its youth, reaching, in some cases, a quarter of its total workforce, this in Italy, Spain, and Greece. France and the UK were also struggling with persistently slowing growth and excessive debt. Even Germany's GDP was contracting now, grappling with high energy costs and persistent inflation. And if more tariffs and protectionism were to come in the future, a very likely scenario, what will then happen to this global system? If weakness continues to spread globally, might not protests also spread globally? The global protests of 2019 might even be a minor preview of future global protests, ever more radical, just as the global economy also is starting to falter ever more.

The 2019 *fast-and-furious* global protests might have been paused by the 2020 Covid-19 pandemic, but only temporarily. By 2013, protesting popped up yet again in France, now led by Unions against recent plans to overhaul the pension system and budget cuts. The protests were yet again radical, with Union workers cutting electrical power only to politicians and the wealthy, "while handing out discounted power and gas to the public," as *The Wall Street* reported. It was a novel strategy clearly aimed at undermining the rich *directly*, and pushing for a sort of grassroots redistribution revolt.[276] These were

---

[275] *https://www.wsj.com/articles/chinas-hot-housing-market-begins-to-cool-151609860*

[276] *https://www.wsj.com/articles/french-union-cuts-power-to-pressure-macron-on-*

developments that suggested ever deeper class divisions for such protests. France also here launched a new grassroots strategy called the "Block Everything" Movement, involving blockading highways, setting fires, and disrupting the traffic, much in the way those *fast-and-furious* protests happened back in 2018 and 2019.

In 2025, in Nepal, demonstrators set fire to key government buildings, including the Parliament, Supreme Court, and presidential and prime ministerial residences; all unprecedented actions triggered by deep-seated anger over decades of political corruption, lack of economic opportunities, and a ban on social media. These protesters also went further than they had before, this time toppling Nepal's government, and forcing the dissolution of its parliament. An interim Prime Minister had to be appointed at short notice. Order was only restored via the full mobilization of the Nepali Army, but only to a point. But what was notable here was how, after the government was toppled, thousands of youth used a free instant messaging and social platform, Discord, originally created for video gamers, to set up a server called "Youths Against Corruption," which then grew to over 145,000 members in just four days. This server was then used to hold a "mini-election," nominating Sushila Karki as the country's first female interim Prime Minister. Multiple rounds of informal voting were held on the server to narrow down the choices. Over 10,000 users participated in hours of live-streamed voice, video, and text debates about the country's future. In a final open poll of 7,713 participants, former Supreme Court Chief Justice Sushila Karki won by reportedly crossing a 50% threshold, with 3,833 votes. Only then did protests leaders from the civic group Hami Nepal met with Nepal's Army Chief,

---

pensions-11674815439

General Ashok Raj Sigdel, to present their Discord-nominated candidate. Seeking a stable transition, the military accepted the nomination of the politically neutral Karki, who was then sworn in as Nepal's first female Prime Minister on September 12, 2025. She dissolved Parliament, and prepared for elections in March 2026. While supporters here hailed it as "digital democracy," some questioned the extralegal nature of choosing a national leader via a gaming app. But regardless of this criticism, the intention here was again like the idea of a direct democracy put forth by the Yellow Vests in France back in 2019. This also showed how this notion of a direct democracy was gaining force, perhaps even globally, and should be then be taken seriously, and even seen as a future trend to be watched for in the politics of the future.

In 2025, in Indonesia, thousands of protesters again took to the streets, mostly students, activists, and labor unions. This time they presented six major demands, and among them was the raising of minimum wages, and the ending of outsourcing, and of mass layoffs, and some labor tax reductions. The most radical were the students here, with one group trying to climb the parliament's fence, and then spreading the protest to a nearby shopping district, an expressway, and two railway stations, and causing all manner of disruptions. Again, this was a fast and furious protest. The students here demanded the complete dissolution of the national police due to its violent killing of a demonstrator a few days earlier.

Due to the significant participation of the Gen Z youth leading these 2025 protests, they were soon dubbed the Gen-X protests. They also spread to Madagascar, Morocco, Peru, Togo, and Mexico and were characterized by their speed and radicalism, just as in 2019, and followed a decentralized digital organization, a shared pop-culture symbolism, and a fierce rejection of government and inequality. While varying in triggers, all were unified by this generation's frustration with stagnant living standards and unresponsive political elites.

Political radicalization was clearly not only persisting but, in many regions, intensifying. This trend was driven by a combination of economic instability, the weakening of traditional institutions, and a global shift toward populist movements. The sustained economic hardship and high inflation continued to fuel voter discontent, which often led to the rejection of traditional, moderate parties in favor of alternatives that promise radical change. It also led to punishing any incumbent party or leader, seeing them a responsible for the continued worsening of the situation.

There was also a voter trend to view political opponents as not just wrong, but immoral, and even as a threat to the nation, with this type of hostility rising significantly over the last decade, and with no signs of reversing. And the rapid deployment of AI, and the persistence of social media algorithms might also be creating a certain information disorder, which then reinforced echo chambers and encouraged political leaders to adopt more radical rhetoric to appeal to their bases. The ongoing rise of far-right was also creating ever more internal pressures in the US, complicating the ability to lead with moderate institutions and polices as used before. This might mean then that the entire postwar order in which we live in might be due for an overhaul.

What might come in its stead then?

Since radicalism has reached levels not seen since the 1960s, one way forward might be to push forth ever more pure forms of democratic rule, such as building a *direct democracy,* like in ancient Athens, a form of government where citizens participate directly in decision-making and lawmaking rather than through elected representatives. We've seen this already being demanded among the 2019 Yellow Vests, and used in practice by the 2025 Gen-Z protesters in Nepal, who even elected a leader then via the gaming app Discord. All important decisions in the future might even be made via full internet assemblies, which might then become the only source of sovereignty and legitimacy of any future government and policy. People today might be just too educated, too literate, and too well-informed to give up authority anymore to a representative. This would not spell the end of democracy, but a continuation of democracy as a direct democracy, much like Ancient classical Greek direct democracy perhaps. Citizens here would then make all decisions on war, foreign policy, and legislation by a simple majority vote, and in a virtual general assembly, and no longer by representatives, which are no longer trusted. It would be *only* the citizens then that would decide everything, and decide on them via a direct vote.

6. THE PERSISTENCE OF DEMOCRACY

Aristotle once wrote: "Where the middle class is numerous, there least occur factions and divisions among citizens."[277] In keeping the *balance* between the rich and the "less educated" poor, as Aristotle put it, the middle classes thus prevented democracy from degenerating into anarchy. It was an old idea. The middle was what kept the whole together. No middle classes; no democracy.

But what happens if the middle classes were to fall apart then in America? Would its democracy then survive?

According to the Pew Research Center, middle-income households in America fell from 62% in 1970, to just 43% in 2014.[278] Once a proud middle class nation, the US has now become a two-tier society, with an ever-deepening split

---

[277] *https://plato.stanford.edu/entries/aristotle-politics/*

[278] *http://www.pewsocialtrends.org/2015/12/09/the-american-middle-class-is-losing-ground/*
https://news.gallup.com/poll/392708/middle-class-identification-steady.aspx
"Middle- and upper-middle class identification remains lower than it was before the Great Recession. Since then, Americans have been more likely to call themselves members of the working or lower class."

between its *haves* and *have nots*. This started in 1973, as Union and manufacturing jobs were permanently lost, and lost too where the benefits, security, and long vacations that came with them. Unionization has now (2018) then fallen by more than half, to just 11.5%. Today, most jobs are either at the high end or low end of the pay grade.[279] This left Americans struggling at the bottom of a mostly gig economy. And this shows up also in surveys. By 2017, for instance, almost half of Americans lacked a spare $400 for an emergency. The year after that, almost half couldn't afford basic expenses like rent or food.[280] And after the 2020 Covid-19 emergency, almost 20% had lost all their savings, and "a third of those making less than $50,000 had their entire financial cushion wiped out," as an article in *Bloomberg* magazine explained it.[281]

This waning of the middle-income crowd is also structural, and starting since the mid-1970s. According to the RAND Corporation, for instance, between 1975 and 2018, the bottom 90% part of America were losing an *excess* of $2.5 *trillion* dollars income *every single year* to the top 1%. This *excess* loss has now added up to $107.5 *trillion* dollars, the equivalent of paying $1,144 dollars *extra* every month to every working man and woman in the country for the next 43 years, and still leave the top 1% of Americans as filthy rich as they have always been.[282] Again, this was *excess* loss, all of it *on top* of the regular

---

[279] *https://www.nytimes.com/.../recovery-has-created-far-more-low-wage-jobs-than-better*
https://www.washingtonpost.com/business/2018/10/09/its-better-be-born-rich-than-talented/?noredirect=on&utm_term=.0783528ec4a1

[280] *https://www.washingtonpost.com/news/wonk/wp/2016/05/25/the-shocking-number-of-americans-who-cant-cover-a-400-expense*
http://money.cnn.com/2018/05/17/news/economy/us-middle-class-basics-study/index.html

[281] *https://www.bloomberg.com/news/articles/2021-10-13/almost-20-of-u-s-households-lost-entire-savings-during-covid*

[282] *https://time.com/5888024/50-trillion-income-inequality-america/*

earnings of the 1%. These are absolutely shocking numbers.

Furthermore, much of this *excess* money was gained by keeping wages down for decades. Between 1973 and 2013, the average pay for US workers rose only by 9%, while their productivity rose by a whopping 74%. Had wages kept pace with productivity, today's federal minimum wage should be *at least* $18 dollars an hour, and not the misally $7.25 minimum we see today (2023).[283] This was deadly to the middle classes, which have only seen a rapid collapse during this period.

But with America's middle-income earners now largely falling apart, will America then devolve into some sort of anarchy?[284]

Probably not.

For starters, the problem of democracy is much older than just the loss of middle-income earners since the mid-1970s. Democracy in America has actually been losing ground for at least a century now, if not much longer. Data shows this. Back in the 1930s, for instance, 74% of Americans still believed democracy as "essential" for the country. But by the 1940s, 50s, and 60s, and especially after the 1980s, this number fell to a mere 32%. It was a dramatic drop. But it also means that democracy here lost support *both* when the middle classes were still growing in the 50s and 60s, and when they began contracting —during the 1980s, and beyond. It's not so simple to link the fall of democracy just to the economy and inequality. Growing or shrinking, support for democracy has only kept falling. It means the loss of support here had to come from somewhere else.

Looking at US history, we find that this decline in support for democracy started some 150 years ago. Using voter turnout

---

[283] *https://www.epi.org/publication/charting-wage-stagnation/*

[284] *https://www.npr.org/2017/04/04/522554630/francis-fukuyama-on-why-liberal-democracy-is-in-trouble*

rates as our guide, it's possible to look back 200 years. (Before the 1930s there are no reliable opinion polls.) Surprisingly, data shows a decline starting since the second half of the 19th Century, with voting turnouts here peaking in the *1840s*, and then, only falling in later times. For a while, they stayed at around 80%, but this only until 1900. After that, the rates again start to fall, and even faster this time, entering what could be called America's democracy long-term decline, later falling even into the very lowly 50% and 60% marks we see today.[285]

As *The Economist* magazine put it: America's "erosion of confidence in government and public institutions [has been advancing] over many years."[286]

But *why this long-term erosion*? Short answer: because of the fundamental changes in the world of US politics and business. The point at which this long-term erosion coincides almost exactly with the moment America embarked in its first lasting *overseas* imperial war, the 1898 Spanish-American War. We took Guam, the Philippines, and Puerto Rico, a watershed war for America. But it was also met with massive resistance, even public outcry, with opposition forces founding America's Anti-imperialist League in 1898. Every major US intellectual then engaged in this debate. And as one such anti-imperialist put it that year: "The [US] policy of imperialism threatens to change the temper of our people and to put us into a permanent attitude of arrogance, testiness, and defiance towards other nations. Once we enter the field of international conflict as a great military and naval power, we shall be one more bully among bullies. She shall only add one more to the list of

---

[285] *http://www.people-press.org/2015/11/23/1-trust-in-government-1958-2015/*
Voter participation also dropped from 66.8% in 1960, to 54.9% in 2012.
http://www.presidency.ucsb.edu/data/turnout.php
Also see: *https://youtu.be/mGBF6kuvuQ8*

[286] *https://www.vox.com/world/2017/1/25/14385728/economist-intelligence-unit-american-democracy-2016*

oppressors of mankind."[287]

The unpopularity of the Spanish-American War could be seen also in the stiff opposition it faced in Congress: the declaration of war against Spain only passed by the slimmest of margins —just two votes.

It was still a serious break with tradition. Back then, the US still did not yet see itself as an imperial nation. The US Secretary of State, John Quincy Adams, for instance, back in 1921 had even warned: "America... goes not abroad, in search of monsters to destroy. She is the well-wisher to the freedom and independence of all... America's glory is not dominion, but liberty." Quincy Adams also added that if the US did not abide by such basic ideals, "the fundamental maxims of her policy would insensibly change from liberty to force.... She might become the dictatress of the world. She would be no longer the ruler of her own spirit."[288]

Prophetic words.

And, of course, this was exactly what happened. With the Spanish-American War the country opened a new chapter, a new, long path of ever-larger conflicts and interventions abroad, eventually leading into the global power it is today. In the words again of Quincy Adams, the US became indeed *the dictatress of the world*, and even more importantly, *no longer the ruler of her own spirit.*

This "spirit" took yet another massive hit in 1900, with its "corporate revolution," when corporate profits now became, *by law*, the only consideration in running large, stocked-owned companies, with stock-holders here no longer taking part in the company's daily operations. As the historian Roger Osborn put it, this new system made it so that the "managers of any corporation were obliged by law to maximize the value of the

[287] Quoted in: *https://youtu.be/mGBF6kuvuQ8*

[288] *https://loveman.sdsu.edu/docs/1821secofstateJQAdmas.pdf*

shareholders' stocks, removing any obligation (or permission) for the management to act in the wider interests of society."[289] It was a revolution, indeed, but one that brought America's business world under a ruthless system that seemed to spare no one, or have on end other than greed.

And then came a third devastating factor undermining democracy: the 1913 creation of the Federal Reserve System, the country's central bank in all but in name. Americans had never liked central banks. Already in 1813, President Thomas Jefferson had warned about them: "I believe that banking institutions are more dangerous to our liberties than standing armies." He even took the time here to do some forecasting: "If the American people ever allow private banks to control the issue of their currency, first by inflation, then by deflation, the banks and corporations that will grow up around (these banks) will deprive the people of all property until their children wake up homeless on the continent their fathers conquered." Jefferson also pointed out here that to keep this from happening: "The issuing power of currency shall be taken from the banks and restored to the people, to whom it properly belongs."[290] Clearly, Jefferson would have disapproved of the Federal Reserve.

But this central bank faced considerable political opposition in Congress. It was so unpopular that big banks couldn't even use the term "bank" anymore, thus turning words like "reserve" and "system" to make it sound like a federation-type of thing with 12 different branches: one in New York, Boston, Philadelphia, Cleveland, Richmond, Atlanta, Chicago, St. Louis, Minneapolis, Kansas City, Dallas, and San Francisco. It make it

---

[289] Osborne, Roger. *Civilization. A New History of the Western World.* New York, NY: Pegasus Books, 2006, pp. 394-395. The US Steel Corporation appeared in 1900.

[290] *https://www.businessinsider.com/thomas-jefferson-wanred-americans-to-beware-of-the-banks-2011-11*

look decentralized, even democratic. But it was, in fact, as centralized as could be, with ultimate power in the hands of the core banks based in New York City, where it still stealthily still resides. Even President Wilson, the one that signed the Federal Reserve into law, once remarked: "I am a most unhappy man. I have unwittingly ruined my country... We have come to be one of the worst ruled, one of the most completely controlled and dominated Governments in the civilized world no longer a Government by free opinion, no longer a Government by conviction and the vote of the majority, but a Government by the opinion and duress of a small group of dominant men."[291] Since then, this "system" has been reviled by both Right *and* Left. One rightwing economist, Murray Rothbard, for instance, said of the Federal Reserve, it is "virtually in total control of the nation's vital monetary system," and "accountable to no one; has no budget; it is subject to no audit; and no Congressional committee knows of, or can truly supervise, its operations."[292] A power on to itself.

From the Left, Franklin Roosevelt was even blunter: "Government by organized money is just as dangerous as Government by organized mob."[293]

Not surprisingly, such changes —the trifecta of the 1898 Spanish-American War; the rise of the 1900 mandated profit-seeking corporations; and the 1913 creation of the Federal Reserve—, coincided almost exactly with the historical drop in voter turnout rates, falling to 50% since 1900, all of it for the first time in its history, and which has not recovered to this very day. There was, it's true, a slight recovery during World War II (1941-1945), and then during some moments in the Cold War (1945-1991), oscillating up and down somewhat, but

---

[291] *https://www.ourrepubliconline.com/Quote/709*

[292] *https://mises.org/library/case-against-fed*

[293] *http://docs.fdrlibrary.marist.edu/od2ndst.html*

remaining always between 50% and 60%,[294] and, thus, with the old high 80% or higher rates from the 19th Century never ever to come back, not even after the massive expansion of the US middle classes during the 1950s and 60s.

One author, Matt Stoller, aptly called this long period with such low turnout rates, "the 100-year war between monopoly power and democracy," a struggle that, by the way, she feels continues to this day.[295]

But was this decline truly a rejection of the people with the idea of democracy, or was it just the result of the elites hijacking democracy via that trifecta of self-empowering of the top 1% elites in the country?

Will democracy fall apart?

The elites never liked democracies. Back in 1814, one of the most conservative of the framers of the Constitution, President John Adams, had written: "Democracy never lasts long. It soon wastes, exhausts and murders itself. There was never a democracy that did not commit suicide."[296] Also according to John Adams, this was because once people are free they divide into factions, and these factions then turn against each other, leading to an infighting that will then ruin any republic. President James Maddison agreed. Democracy, he said, was doomed. "Men are ambitious, vindictive, and rapacious," he wrote just a few years earlier, in 1787, in the *Federalist Papers*. And the only way to stop them from chaos was to limit their power by "saving" them from their own wickedness and vile

---

[294] *http://www.electproject.org/2016g*
https://www.dailykos.com/stories/2019/2/11/1833450/-True-Democracies-ALWAYS-Fail-Do-You-Know-Why
https://www.penguinrandomhouse.com/books/307217/the-emergency-state-by-david-c-unger/9781101560327/

[295] Stoller, Matt. *Goliath: The 100-Year War Between Monopoly Power and Democracy*. New York, NY: Simon & Schuster, 2019.

[296] *http://www.john-adams-heritage.com/quotes/*

penchant for anarchy. But who could "save" them? Well, the more enlightened folk, of course, —the elites, the rich, the "educated" lucky at the top.[297]

But, again, this is not something much supported by history. Contrary to John Adams and James Madison, democracies rarely fall apart on their own. In fact, they usually remaining relatively stable over long periods of time, if allowed to. The ancient Athenian democracy, for instance, lasted for no less than 189 years, almost two centuries, and only fell apart after Athens was invaded by an outside, non-democratic power, Sparta, backed by the equally anti-democratic Persian Empire. Democracy, thus, was destroyed not by internal anarchy, but by anti-democratic outsider powers bent on getting rid of its "bad" example.

Contrary to popular belief, Athens was *not* the birthplace of democracy. Democracies appeared even *before* the classical period in Greece, although little is known about them. But even if this is dismissed, history still shows how Greece's first "classical" democracy was not Athens, but, very likely, its neighboring city-state of Argos, a smaller city located in the Peloponnesus, some 58 miles west of Athens by sea. Confirmed by both Thucydides and Aristotle, yet generally ignored by textbooks, Argos' was also far more radical as a democracy than that of Athens. Argos, for instance, eliminated of the entire aristocratic class, some 1,200 people —the equivalent of a *few million* of the richest and most powerful Americans today. Furthermore, Argos incorporated all slaves and *gumnetes* — people between free and slave— as full citizens. Argos also made its army the best equipped, and never defeated, not even by the mighty Spartans.[298] Finally, Argos' democracy lasted

---

[297] *https://www.dailykos.com/stories/2019/2/11/1833450/-True-Democracies-ALWAYS-Fail-Do-You-Know-Why*
[298] *https://assets.cambridge.org/97805218/43317/excerpt/9780521843317_*

much longer, perhaps for a total of 800 years, falling only after it was invaded by the much larger, non-democratic armies of Macedon. Again, democracy was not something that broke from the inside. It only fell to a foreign invasion and conquest. Argos might even be an example of the opposite: that the more inclusive and radical democracy is, the more successful, stable, and lasting it might be.

It's true Rome's democratic institutions indeed fell without any foreign invasion, something that has been exploited over and over again by pro-elite thinkers bent on discrediting it. But unlike Argos or Athens, ancient Rome was never a democracy. It was a republic; and one dominated *from the start* by the elites, the *patricians*, who controlled most, if not all top decision-making offices in this republic, chief among them, the Senate. And yet, even in such difficult circumstances, Rome still managed to remain a republic with limited democratic institutions for 482 years, and was also able to preside over its largest expansion, including much of the Mediterranean.[299] Even limited democratic institutions seemed to allow for an extra oomph to expansion.

The only truly democratic institution in ancient Rome was its Tribunes, charged with defending commoners: small farmers, workers, regular folk living in the city and the surrounding farmland. But Tribunes were never top decision-makers. Worse, after the Punic Wars (264-146 BCE), the Tribunes lost almost all their power as Rome was flooded with cheap enslaved labor, mostly put to work in vast estates owned by the top 1%. This vast new captured "slave army" of laborers

---

excerpt.pdf

[299] *http://theweek.com/articles/660915/america-now-looks-like-rome-before-fall-republic* During the empire, Rome hardly expanded its borders beyond where they had been during the republic. It only permanently took Mauritania and Britannia, more or less Dacia, and, for a while only, Armenia, Mesopotamia, and Assyria, which it didn't keep for long.

even further reduced the influence of farmers in politics, eventually opening the path for the powerful patricians to take over total control over economy and government. At one point, some 40% of the population in the Italian heartland of Rome were all slaves.[300]

Rome's republic, thus, did not fall due to the "anarchy" of commoners. It fell apart under the monopolization of power by its wealthy elites.

Roman democratic institutions, while they existed, seemed to have led towards *more* stability, not less. Numbers tell the story. Most of the Roman expansion happened while Rome was still a republic. The expansion only slowed during the latter part of its history, when it fell into its imperial period. This was also the period marked by the most instability, and by the infamous cruelty of its many cruel emperors. During this last 283 years of empire, Rome had 59 emperors, each lasting, on average, a little more than four years. Worse, 62% of these died violent deaths, mostly via assassination.[301] Perhaps the true story here is that democracy was the secret ingredient for its exceptional expansion, and that later elite-dominated, anti-democratic rule was what caused Rome to fall into its brutal, violent, cruel, unstable imperial times. Elite-rule, thus, didn't "save" its people from anarchy. It might have even done the exact opposite: it created that hellish world of oppression which was then called *strength*, *order*, and *stable* rule.

Some might argue that the later republics of Florence in the Renaissance, are a good example of democracy falling into chaos at the hands of the people. But just like with ancient Rome, Florence was not a full democracy, just a republic with

---

[300] Harper, Kyle. *Slavery in the Late Roman World, AD 275–425*. Cambridge University Press, 2011, pp. 58–60. Some Roman commoners —plebeians— gained higher offices than that of the Tribunes after 287 BCE. But these were enriched plebeians, which were, in terms of class, not even plebeians anymore.

[301] *https://www.nature.com/articles/s41599-019-0366-y*

some democratic institutions in it. And, just like in Rome, in spite of being largely elite-dominated, Florence still managed to last for 415 years as a republic, lasting almost as long as the Roman Republic had done a millennia earlier. Florence's democratic institutions also did not fall due to internal "anarchy," but to an outsider, a non-democratic invading army, that of the Spaniards in 1530 —which, by the way, also ended Florence's much admired period of innovation in politics, sciences, and the Arts, all of it, almost certainly, the result of the loss of its basic democratic liberties, all squashed by the invading and authoritarian Spaniards.[302]

Fortunately for democracy, today's modern industrial democracies seem to be even more resilient than the ancient powers of Rome, or Renaissance Florence. In England, and then Britain, for instance, democratic institutions have lasted, so far, for 700 years, exceeding the 482 years of the Roman Republic, and of Florence's 415 republican years, and even approaching that record-long 800 years held by Argos' fully democratic rule. England's core democratic institution, the House of Commons, was first created in 1341, and, with the centuries, has only *gained* influence, especially in the last 380 years. Britain's House has also grown ever more democratic in the industrial age. By 1884, for instance, most of adult males had gained the right to vote. Even during the tumultuous world wars and the 1930s Great Depression, Britain still expanded its democratic institutions, reaching almost universal suffrage in the 1930s, when it also shifted to the Left politically.[303]

---

[302] The early rise of *il popolo* (the people) in Florence was facilitated by guilds. But being a pre-industrial society, Florence faced the limitations of guilds as political representation and their inability to expand popular enfranchisement. See: Osborne, *op. cit.*, pp. 184-209.

[303] *https://www.ice.cam.ac.uk/course/wind-change-post-war-britain-1945-1965 https://www.zmescience.com/science/news-science/democracy-failing-west-18092017/*

America might be following this same trend. Its democratic institutions are already more than 235 years old, and this *only* counting since the US Constitution 1788 ratification.[304] One might stretch this way further back, all the way to the early compacts of the first European settlers, such as, for instance, the 1620 Mayflower Compact, settled more than a century earlier, and which would bring the total age of democratic institutions in America to almost 400 years. Ever since democracy in the US has only been expanding, at least formally. By the 1830s, for instance, voting rights were given to most White men over the age of 21. And by the 1840s and 1850s, it spread even further by removing all property restrictions on all its White male citizens —the first large nation to ever do so. And in 1865, it finally abolished slavery, opening the path for Black Americans to gain full voting rights, even though that was later squashed by the Jim Crow laws. By the 1870s, the US somewhat democratized its Senate, too —although today it's still very much the seat of the nation's top plutocrats. By 1920, the right to vote was now extended to all women. And in 1924, it was also extended to Native-Americans. And by 1964, the US finally got rid of its Jim Crow laws. And by the 1960s and 70s, as US historian Alexander Keyssar might put it, "the right to vote was effectively nationalized for the first time," with Keyssar also adding here that by the "early 1970s, the United States, formally at least, already had something very close to universal suffrage."[305]

There are still many obstacles. The US, for instance, still has a very anti-democratic Electoral College; a very anti-

---

http://www.pewglobal.org/2017/10/16/globally-broad-support-for-representative-and-direct-democracy/

[304] *https://www.weforum.org/agenda/2019/08/countries-are-the-worlds-oldest-democracies/*

[305] Keyssar Alexander. *The Right to Vote: The Contested History of Democracy in the United States.* New York: NY, Basic Books, 2009, p. 224.

democratic Senate —giving disproportionate weight to smaller states over more populous ones—; an anti-democratic gerrymandering; and the pesky issues with filibusters, presidential pardons, and lack of voter protection. Worse still, in real terms, 70% of Americans today are completely excluded from all top political decisions.[306] The Very Long Shift to the Right has, for the last 50 years, turned the clock backwards even on voter rights in general, as pointed out, for instance, by politician Stacy Abrams in her book *Our Time is Now.*

But does this mean America's democracy is doomed?

Again, not necessarily. Support for democracy may still be waning at the polls, as so many seem to like to point out, but there is also still no other clear alternative. Support for democracy may be as low as 30% today, even under 20%. But support for authoritarian rule is even lower, at just 7%.[307] Finally, most Americans want more democracy, not less. One data-based study, for instance, found that even rightwing populists —appealing to everyday folk ignored by the elites— are not necessarily a hindrance against democracy, and that they prefer democracy to most other forms of government.[308] Also, one Gallup poll found that 61% of Americans today want the anti-democratic Electoral College gone —an institution that, by the way, only survives because 77% of Republican voters still protect it wholeheartedly.[309]

---

306 *https://www.washingtonpost.com/news/worldviews/wp/2017/01/26/america-is-no-longer-a-full-democracy-a-new-study-warns/?utm_term=.b4701eb2917b*

307 *http://www.people-press.org/2015/11/23/1-trust-in-government-1958-2015/*

308 Andrej Zaslove, Bram Geurkink, Kristof Jacobs, and Agnes Akkerman. "Power to the people? Populism, democracy, and political participation: a citizen's perspective," in *West European Politics*, 2021, 44:4, 727-751, DOI: 10.1080/01402382.2020.1776490

309 Between 1967 and 1980... 58% to 80% approved an amendment to "do away with the Electoral College and base the election of a president on the total vote cast throughout the nation." For more data, see: *https://news.gallup.com/poll/320744/americans-support-abolishing-electoral-college.aspx*

Lastly, there is the matter of the Rule of Law —legal principles limiting arbitrary power. Support here is still also strong, enjoying also a robust tradition that goes back some 800 years, at least if we count since the English 1215 *Magna Carta*. Either way, Americans today still trust judges more than the President. One example of this: at the very height of his popularity, back in 2017, President Donald Trump was still not trusted as much as US judges.[310] And this was not just an abstraction: it translated into actual political practice, with members of Trump's *own* party later resisting his attempts to overturn election 2020 results. As *The New York Times* reported back then: "key states Republicans were critical in resisting Trump's election narrative." *Republicans* here even certified the election *against* Trump. They "repudiated a president of their own party," as *The New York Times* also explained, even while facing serious pressures from its president and many followers.[311] The Rule of Law may be a very embattled tradition, but may not yet be entirely out for the picture.

And yet the core question still remains: will US democracy survive?

The answer, again, is it probably will.

We've seen serious attempts at overthrowing democracy before. In 1933, for instance, ultra-rich Americans tried to overthrow President Roosevelt in a plan now known as the White House Putsch, which failed when its leader, retired General Smedley Butler, decided to turn in the conspirators,

[310] Support for judges was 53% in 2017, well above Trump's approval ratings. *https://www.theguardian.com/commentisfree/2017/feb/11/americans-arent-attached-democracy-rule-law*
http://www.pewglobal.org/2017/10/16/globally-broad-support-for-representative-and-direct-democracy/
http://www.bbc.com/news/blogs-echochambers-27074746

[311] *https://www.nytimes.com/2020/11/28/us/politics/trump-republicans-election-results.html*

denouncing them all to Congress.[312] Butler preferred the Rule of Law, again suggesting a certain strength of this tradition, even under the very embattled conditions of the then Great Depression.

It should be remembered that during this same time, the putsches of Benito Mussolini in Italy, and later of Adolf Hitler in Germany, had both succeeded. In the US did they not only succeed, but the country even shifted to the Left in a major way under the New Deal. Other countries with stronger Rules of Law, also fared well. Canada, Britain, Australia, New Zealand, Holland, and France, all avoided far-right putsches, and shifted, just as in the US, towards the Left —unless, of course, they were invaded, as was the case of Holland or France, falling into the hands of Nazi-driven far-right leaders.

Today's Right might seem like an unstoppable force. It's only been advancing for 50 years. Will today's weaker support for democracy then lead towards a forever far-right shift in the US?

Again, not likely.

A fall in support for democracy does not necessarily mean people don't want democracy anymore. As argued before, it might mean people are reacting to the hijacking by elites of the country's power, a sign that they might feel they don't have *enough* democracy, and want more of it, not less —even if it's not always picked in the way the surveys are usually conducted.

Second, the education levels have grown immensely compared to 100 years ago. This might seem unimportant. But this change has been massive. Higher education among women, in particular, has exploded. Back in the 1930s, few women had a college degree —barely 3.8%. But by the early

---

[312] *https://www.washingtonpost.com/history/2021/01/13/fdr-roosevelt-coup-business-plot/*

2020s this number was reaching 38.5%.[313] According to the book *All the Single Ladies* by Rebecca Traister, argued that, "the decline of marriage over the last generation has helped create an emerging voting bloc of unmarred women that is profoundly reshaping the American electorate," shifting it also towards democracy.[314] Furthermore, women in America have gone from being 20 percentage points "more Republican" in 1994, to more than 30 percentage points "more Democrat" in 2018, according to *Wall Street Journal* data,[315] a major shift. And together with the higher levels of education, women point at even more political participation. According to a study in the *American Political Science Review*, education tends to increase political participation, including among the educated *poor*.[316] It suggests democracy may actually gain ground in the future, not lose it, especially if we have more educated poor, as we have today.

But there's a third, even more clear reason why leftwing pro-democracy political participation might be on the rise: new generations, all clearly shifting to the Left. Millennials —born since 1982— are more liberal than GenXers. As the *Washington Post* famously put it, in 2016, 80% of Millennials voted for the socialist candidate Bernie Sanders during the Democratic primaries and caucuses of that year. And among those under 30 years, more voted for Sanders than for Donald Trump *and*

---

[313] *https://www.infoplease.com/us/education/educational-attainment-sex-1910-2020*

[314] Traister, Rebecca. *All the Single Ladies. Unmarried Women and the Rise of an Independent Nation.* New York, NY: Simon & Shuster, 2016, p. 31.

[315] *https://www.wsj.com/articles/the-yawning-divide-that-explains-american-politics-1540910719*

[316] Urbanization also might be correlated with intensified political demands. See: *https://www.cambridge.org/core/journals/american-political-science-review/article/urbanization-and-political-demand-making-political-participation-among-the-migrant-poor-in-latin-american-cities/3CA214D2BE108981B5B0EDE95BE882BB*

Hillary Clinton *combined*.[317] Gen Zs, or Zoomers —born after 1995—, are more left-leaning than the Millennials, and as these generations grow and mature, so will the vote for the Left, and, most likely, too, in favor of more democracy.

But what if a depression were to hit America? Might this not impoverish the middle class, radicalize America, and perhaps even push it into totalitarianism?

Again, not likely. Depressions have actually resulted in *major shifts to the Left*, not to the Right. As this book argued in Chapter 2, the Depression of 1837 fuelled a big shift to the Left, as did the Long Depression in 1873. Finally, the 1930s Great Depression saw a major shift to the Left under Roosevelt's New Deal. Depressions, thus, move the US to the Left, and in a major way.

Why would it be any different today?

Americans are even more educated than at any time in the past. Why wouldn't they not participate *more* in politics?

Under such conditions, a future depression will be far more radical than that of the 1930s, especially since younger generations, especially women and Blacks, are already shifting more to the Left *today*. But it's also reasonable to suggest that this new shift to the Left will not be focused so much on cultural wars, peace, and/or global justice issues like in the 1960s. This new shift to the Left will be one focused on hard, immediate demands, with Christian crusaders, say, calling for the abolishing of the Federal Reserve; Black socialists calling for the end of violent policing; militant feminists calling for universal health care; populists calling for wealth caps; homeless calling for housing redistribution; Unions calling for

---

[317] *https://www.washingtonpost.com/news/the-fix/wp/2016/06/20/more-young-people-voted-for-bernie-sanders-than-trump-and-clinton-combined-by-a-lot https://www.theatlantic.com/politics/archive/2016/02/the-liberal-millennial-revolution/470826/*

capital controls; and everyone calling for the end of globalization, "free trade," immigration, and in favor of rent control, expanded food programs, even universal basic income.

A depression would definitively flip things on its head, but not necessarily in the same way everywhere in the world. Back in the 1930s, for instance, democracies and major shifts to the Left only happened in the countries with the longest democratic. Such were the cases of the US, Canada, Britain, Australia, and New Zealand. The UK was a somewhat more mixed case. It remained conservative, but its leftwing Labour Party strengthened its power over local organizations, opening the path to a more effective presence in London since 1934, and then nationally by 1935, which then led to its entry into the wartime coalition government under Winston Churchill in 1940, and then to a considerable success at the local level during all that decade. Countries with shorter or weaker democratic institutions, like, say, Italy or Germany, fell completely apart politically during the 1930s, shifting to the very far Right, and splitting the world into two camps: those with extreme forms of rightwing regimes, such as fascism and Nazism in Italy and in Germany, respectively; and then the camp of the liberal-leaning democracies, such as that led by FRD's 1930s America. A similar thing might happen if another economic depression hits the world during the late-2020s, or in the early to mid-2030s. Those countries with stronger democratic backgrounds, such as the US, UK, Canada, Australia, and New Zealand, and perhaps now Switzerland, Holland, Belgium, France, and Austria, will likely remain democratic, and even shift to the Left in a significant way. The Scandinavian countries, plus Finland might go the same way. Germany might also remain democratic, and even shift to the Left, at least its *western* half, the one with the longest and most solid democratic tradition.

Outside of Europe, countries with 60 to 70 year democracy traditions may also have a medium chance at keeping their democracies. Israel, Costa Rica, Japan, Colombia, India, and Jamaica, for instance, might be on this list,[318] but they might also turn out to be somewhat problematic, too. Israel's younger generations are already turning rightwards, not leftwards, pushing the country's politics into combining elections with an institutionalized favoritism towards one dominant ethnic group, what is now many times called an *ethno-democracy*. India might be going in this same direction, basing it on its powerful Hindu majority. Hungary is already being called an *ethno-democracy*, and no longer considered a democracy by most western European leaders. Japan might continue with its elections, but under the dominant party system that it has had under its Liberal Democratic Party model since 1955.

Some countries may not make the 60-year mark, but might show some promise as mixed-democracies inside a future depression. Mexico, for instance, may be well under this 60-year threshold, but might also continue with elections under a liberal-authoritarian system, as it also did back during the 1930s depression.

And even among those countries with younger democracies, like Brazil or South Korea, democracy has shown a notable degree of resilience. After a rightwing attempted coup by former Brazilian president Jair Bolsonaro following his 2022 election loss, he was sentenced to 27 years and three months for leading a conspiracy to keep him in power, which included plans to assassinate then President Luiz Inácio Lula da Silva. And after violating house arrest conditions —including tampering with an ankle monitor— Bolsonaro was moved to a federal police jail cell in November 2025. Also, multiple high-

---

318 *https://www.weforum.org/agenda/2019/08/countries-are-the-worlds-oldest-democracies/*

ranking allies, including military officers, were also sentenced to long prison terms for their roles in the conspiracy. Previously banned from running for office until 2030, this conviction further solidified the end of his political career, forcing his allies to search for a new leader for the far-right movement, and, in the process, giving more credibility to the rule of law in Brazil, and its democratic institutions.

And in December 2024, in South Korea then President Yoon Suk-yeol, facing a 'lame-duck' presidency due to an opposition-controlled National Assembly that blocked his policies and budget, Yoon declared emergency martial law, and accused the opposition Democratic Party (DPK) of being "anti-state" forces collaborating with North Korean communists. Yoon then ordered the military to paralyze the National Assembly, and planned to arrest key opposition leaders, including the leader of the Democratic Party. But Parliament immediately overturned the order, and the Constitutional Court unanimously upheld his impeachment, and in 2026 he has sentenced to life in prison for insurrection. He also became the first sitting president arrested in South Korean history. Other officials also received long prison terms. Again, this showed the democratic resilience in a country that didn't even had that long a democracy, and despite this severe crisis, the quick, non-violent, and constitutional reversal of the martial law by the National Assembly highlighted the strength of South Korean democratic institutions.

Neither cases in Brazil or in South Korea here were a clear guarantee that such younger democracies will always prevail, but they do show that in spite of the ever-deepening inequality and polarizing politics, democracy can still be surprisingly resilient, and even rise as the only acceptable solution in much divided countries going through serious political turbulence.

It's very likely that other nations with little to no democratic traditions will likely remain authoritarian, including countries like Russia and China, were self-proclaimed life-long leaders today, such as Russia's Vladimir Putin, and China's Xi Jinping, have made the idea of any future transition to a democracy very unlikely.

But regardless of where countries may go ideologically, Left or Right, all nations will turn away from globalism, and "free trade," and embrace its opposite: protectionism, capital controls, and mass public reliefs, in some cases perhaps under strict government control, as happened, say, during the 1930s Soviet Union or Nazi Germany. Insularity will be the norm. America's isolationism, for instance, will return, as it's already doing today —as seen, for instance, with Trump's 2025 tariffs wars. Even autarky might make a comeback in this future. The world will also turn 100% against immigration. Mass deportations can already be seen with the 2021 expulsion of thousands of Haitians under US President Biden, and with President Trump's 2025 harsh anti-immigrant polices.

The era of "global" orders will be over, and the world will turn into an almost unrecognizable place from what it is today.

Again, this is hard to believe today. But the last 50 years have been unprecedented. They have been the only case of such a Very Long Shift to the Right in all of US history. But this does not mean it can last forever. To use the old rubber band analogy, this extremely long shift to the Right has likely stretched this rubber band way too far, and will, at some point, end in an extreme shift back in the opposite direction: towards the Left, especially in the case of a new depression. This new shift to the Left will be sudden, unexpected, and radical, with the American politics already showing signs of being primed for it in the way of the recent advances of its democratic socialists. All that needs to happen is an economic depression to trigger this massive change, and let it reach its full political manifestation.

The Economist magazine in 2022 was already arguing that: "you might expect politics to move left, if only in reaction to the mainly center-right governments that dominated rich democracies during the previous decade." *The Economist* also argued that, "Some years have a way of giving countries, even continents, a shove in a new direction..." The article posed the following question: "Might 2023 be another such year?"[319] The year 2023 came and went, and there was no big *shove in this new direction*. But the thought is still interesting, hinting as it does at a major change in favor of some kind of Left in the not too distant future.

The *Financial Times* business columnist Rana Foroohar also seemed to agree. She pointed out in one interview how younger generations were now becoming the largest voting and working block in industrial nations, and yet "they don't have any assets to protect." She noted also how these new generations have grown up in what, for them, has always been "a structural declining market," while all the time only accruing huge piles of debt, and without having "anything invested in the old system." Foroohar thus concluded this younger generation, as it begins to dominate the vote of the future, will "really begin to challenge the boomers." She then concluded that the current, old system will "change pretty quickly." She even called this change a "deeper shift" in politics.[320]

The Fourth Turning also explores a similar major cycle, and called also for a major social shift sometime between 2008 and 2030.

The economist Nouriel Roubini —the one that correctly

---

[319] *https://www.economist.com/international/2023/01/01/politics-will-move-further-to-the-left-in-2023*

[320] Rana Foroohar interviewed by Steve Paikin in *The Agenda*, Canada, January 10, 2023. *https://www.youtube.com/watch?v=oAgylzBWxmg*

forecasted the housing bubble of 2008—, also called for a major depression in the mid-2020s. Using yield inversions (when longer-term bonds offer lower yields than short-term debts), analysts here have also found signs of a depression likely hitting in 2026, but with this one being "WORSE than the 1929 and 2008" ones.[321]

The geopolitical expert Peter Zeihan also spoke of a serious drop in capital availability worldwide during 2020-2024. He did not foresee any shift to the Left, to be very clear. But it still fit with most of the forecasts mentioned here: a major downturn in the mid-2020s or early 2030s, leading to a major crisis, and, as the Fourth Turning argued, to a major shift to the Left.

Such forecasts may be hard to believe. Today the Right looks unbeatable, eternal even, while the Left looks powerless, disorganized, even "impotent," "a lost cause," unable to counter most of the many advances of the Right in the last 50 years, as Slavoj Žižek, the leftist philosopher, might put it. Žižek here even warned us of a Left that was seemingly falling into a very lasting state of irrelevance.[322]

But we've seen this movie before. Societies may seem solid, unmovable, but they also have a way of changing dramatically, and in very short time. Back in 1988, for instance, communism seemed eternal, much like the Right today. Back in 1988 communism had a long history, starting at least since the rise of the Soviet Union in 1917, and later, after World War II, spreading its influence to Eastern Europe, all the way from Poland to Albania. Very large communist parties also rose in Italy and France. Communism also spread to India, winning

---

[321] *https://www.gameoftrades.net/blog/2023s-yield-curve-inversion-is-comparable-to-1928-and-2006/*

[322] *https://www.opendemocracy.net/can-europe-make-it/slavoj-zizek-benjamin-ramm/slavoj-i-ek-on-brexit-crisis-of-left-and-future-of-eur*

two important states here, Bihar and Jharkhand in 1947. In 1949, it spread to China, and in later years to North Korea, Cuba, Vietnam, Cambodia, and, in Africa, to Ethiopia, Angola, and Somalia during the 1980s and 90s. Communism then ruled a third of the world, and it was seen as a permanent force in history. *No one* in their right mind would have ever dared in 1988 to forecast its quick and massive fall, followed by a massive shift to the Right all over. And yet this was exactly what happened. In just one year, 1989, communism fell in Eastern Europe, and two years later, in the Soviet Union, too; and then in Yugoslavia, and in Ethiopia and Somalia. China may have continued communist, nominally, but with a very strong capitalist bend at its core. The world had changed, and had done so very *unexpectedly* and *drastically*. *And no one saw it coming.*[323] *Not one* single *expert* foresaw it. In fact, if anyone had made such grandiose claims that same person would have been immediately labeled crazy or high.

But things sometimes change quickly. As an old Russian prime minister, Pyotr Stolypin, put it (allowing for some paraphrasing): "In a century, nothing changes in the country. In a year, everything changes."

History is like this. It's not always linear. And today we are at the very threshold of one of those cycles, and of one of those massive shifts, even if we still can't see it right now. And the cycles of history suggest it will change politics in favor of the Left, and towards more government regulation, and even in a much larger scale than back in the 1930s. It may all sound so impossible today. But so did the fall of the Berlin Wall just before the year 1989.

---

[323] *https://www.ssoar.info/ssoar/bitstream/handle/document/1628/ssoar-2008-cox-1989_and_why_we_got.pdf*

REFERENCES

Accmoglu, Daron and James A. Robinson. *Why Civilizations Fail. The Origins of Power, Prosperity and Poverty.* New York, NY: Crown Publications, 2012.

Abrams, Stacey. *Our Time is Now: Power, Purpose, and the Fight for a Fair America.* New York, NY: Henry Holt & Company, 2020.

Ahamed, Liaquad. *Lords of Finance. The Bankers Who Broke the World.* New York, NY: The Penguin Press, 2009.

Akerlof, George A. and Robert J. Shiller. *Animal Spirits. How Human Psychology Drives the Economy, and Why it Matters for Global Capitalism.* Princeton, NJ: Princeton University Press, 2009.

Alexander, Benjamin F. *Coxey's Army. Popular Protest in the Gilded Age.* Baltimore, MA. John Hopkins University Press, 2015.

Alexander, Brian. *Glass House: The 1% Economy and the Shattering of the All-American Town*. New York, NY: St. Martin Press, 2018.

Allerfeldt, Kristofer (editor). *The Progressive Era in the USA: 1890–1921*. London, UK: Routledge, 2019.

Appelbaum, Eileen, and Rosemary Batt. *The New American Workplace: Transforming Work Systems in the United States*. Ithaca, NY: Cornel University Press, 1994.

Bair, Sheila. *Bull by the Horns: Fighting to Save Main Street from Wall Street*. New York, NY: Free Press, 2012.

Banerjee, Abhijit, and Esther Duflo. *Good Economics for Hard Times*. New York, NY: PublicAffairs, 2019.

Banerjee, Abhijit, and Esther Duflo. *Poor Economics: A Radical Rethinking of the Way to Fight Global Poverty*. New York, NY: PublicAffairs, 2011.

Baptist, Edward E. *The Half Has Never Been Told: Slavery and the Making of American Capitalism*. New York, NY: Basic Books, 2014.

Barioch, Paul. *Economics and World History. Myths and Paradoxes*. Chicago, IL: Chicago University Press, 1993.

Beito, David T. *From Mutual Aid to the Welfare State: Fraternal Societies and Social Services, 1890-1967*. Chapel Hill, NC: The University of North Carolina Press, 2000.

Bell, Daniel. *The End of Ideology. On the Exhaustion of Political Ideas in the Fifties*. New York, NY: Free Press, 1962.

Bernstein, William J. *A Splendid Exchange. How Trade Shaped the World*. New York, NY: Atlantic Monthly Press, 2008.

Bishop, Bill. *The Big Sort: Why the Clustering of Like-Minded America is Tearing Us Apart.* New York, NY: Houghton Mifflin Harcourt Publishing Company, 2009.

Blum, Rachel M. *How the Tea Party Captured the GOP: Insurgent Factions in American Politics.* Chicago, IL: The University of Chicago Press, 2020.

Brinkley, Alan. *Voices of Protests. Huey Long, Father Coughlin, & The Great Depression.* New York, NY: Vintage Books, 1983.

Brown, David S. *Moderates: the Vital Center of American Politics, from the Founding to Today.* Chapel Hill, NC: The University of North Carolina Press, 2016.

Bulter, John Sibley. *Entrepreneurship and Self-Help Among Black Americans: A Reconsideration of Race and Economics.* New York, NY: State University of New York, 2005.

Carney, Timothy P. *Alienated America: Why Some Places Thrive While Others Collapse.* New York, NY: HarperCollins, 2019.

Caryl, Christian. *Strange Rebels: 1979 and the Birth of the 21st Century.* New York, NY: Basic Books, 2013.

Case, Anne, and Angus Deaton. *Deaths of Despair and the Future of Capitalism.* Princeton, NJ: Princeton University Press, 2020.

Desmond, Matthew. *Evicted. Poverty and Profit in the American City.* New York, NY: Crown Publishers, 2016.

De Tocqueville, Alexis. *Democracy in America* (abridged version). New York, NY: HarperPerennial, 1969.

Dubofsky, Melvyn, and Joseph A. McCartin. *Labor in America: A History.* West Sussex, UK: John Wiley & Sons, 2017.

Ehrenreich, Barbara. *Nickel and Dimed. On (Not) Getting By in America.* New York, NY: Henry Holt and Company, 2001.

Faludi, Susan. *Backlash: The Undeclared War Against American Women.* New York, NY: Three Rivers Press, 2006.

Faux, Jeff. *The Servant Economy: Where America's Elite is Sending the Middle Class.* West Sussex, UK: John Wiley & Sons, 2012.

Ferguson, Thomas, and Joel Rogers. *Right Turn. The Decline of the Democrats and the Future of American Politics.* New York, NY: Hill and Wang, 1986.

Fisher, Dana R. *American Resistance: From the Women's March to the Blue Wave.* New York, NY: Columbia University Press, 2019.

Fisher, Mark. *Capitalist Realism: Is There No Alternative?* Winchester, UK: Zero Books, 2010.

Foner, Eric. *Reconstruction: America's Unfinished Revolution, 1863–1876.* New York, NY: HarperCollins Publishers, 1988.

Foroohar, Rana. *Makers and Takers: The Rise of Finance and the Fall of American Business.* New York, NY: Currency, 2016.

Frank, Thomas. *What's the Matter with Kansas? How Conservatives Won the Heart of America.* New York, NY: A Metropolitan/Owl Book, 2004.

Frank, Thomas. *The People, No: A Brief History of Anti-Populism.* New York, NY: Metropolitan Books, 2020.

Franks, Tommy. *American Soldier General Tommy Franks.* New York, NY: Regan Books, 2004.

Fraser, Caroline. *Prairie Fires. The American Dreams of Laura Ingalls Wilder*. New York, NY: Metropolitan Books, 2017.

Fredrickson, Caroline. *Under the Bus: How Working Women Are Being Run Over*. New York, NY: The New Press, 2016.

Fukuyama, Francis. *The End of History and the Last Man*. New York, NY: Free Press, 1992.

Gallea, Anthony M. and William Patalon. *Contrarian Investing*. New York, NY: New York Institute of Finance, 1998.

Gelder, Sarah van. *This Changes Everything. Occupy Wall Street and the 99% Movement*. San Francisco, CA: Berrett-Koehler Publishers, 2011.

Gillion, Daniel Q. *The Loud Minority. Why Protests Matter in American Democracy*, Cadiz, KY: Books FYI Inc., 2010.

Gilpin, Robert, and Jean Millis Gilpin. *The Challenge of Global Capitalism. The World Economy in the 21st Century*. Princeton, NJ: Princeton University Press, 2010.

Goldman, David P. *How Civilizations Die (And Why Islam is Dying too)*. Washington, DC: Regnery Publishing, Inc., 2011.

Gordon, Robert. *The Rise and Fall of American Growth*. Princeton, NJ: Princeton University Press, 2016.

Griffin, Edward. *The Creature of Jekyll Island. A Second Look at the Federal Reserve*. New York, NY: American Media, 1994.

Hoffer, Eric. *The True Believer. Thoughts of the Nature of Mass Movements*. New York, NY: Harper Perennial, 2010.

Hudson, Michael. *Killing the Host. How Financial Parasites and Debt Destroy the Global Economy*. Dresden, Germany: Islet-Verlag, 2015.

Hudson, Michael. *...and forgive them their debts: Lending, Foreclosure and Redemption from Bronze Age Finance to the Jubilee Year*. Dresden, Germany: Islet-Verlag, 2018.

Isenberg, Nancy. *White Trash. The 400-Year Untold History of Class in America*. New York, NY: Viking. 2016.

Johnson, Daryl. *Hateland. A Long, Hard Look at America's Extremist Hart*. Amherst, NY; Prometheus Books, 2019.

Johnston, David Cay. *Free Lunch. How the Wealthiest Americans Enrich Themselves at Government Expense (and Stick You with the Bill)*. New York, NY; Portfolio, 2007.

Jones, Robert P. *The End of White Christian America*. New York: NY, Simon & Schuster, 2017.

Judis, John B. *The Populist Explosion. How the Great Recession Transformed American and European Politics*. New York, NY: Columbia Global Reports, 2016.

Kazin, Michael. *What It Took to Win. A History of the Democratic Party*. New York, NY: Farrar, Straus and Giroux, 2022.

Keen, Steven. *Can We Avoid Another Financial Crisis?* New York, NY: Polity Press, 2017.

Keller, Morton. *Affairs of State: Public Life in Late Nineteenth-Century America*. Cambridge, MA: Harvard University Press, 1977.

Keyssar Alexander. *The Right to Vote: The Contested History of Democracy in the United States.* New York: NY, Basic Books, 2009.

Kinzer, Stephen. *The True Flag: Theodore Roosevelt, Mark Twain, and the Birth of American Empire.* New York, NY: Henry Holt & Company, 2017.

Kloppenberg, James T. *Uncertain Victory: Social Democracy and Progressivism in European and American Thought, 1870-1920.* New York, NY: Oxford University Press, 1986.

Kroszner, Randall S., and Robert J. Schiller. *Reforming U.S. Financial Markets. Reflections Before and Beyond Dodd-Frank.* Cambridge, MA: The MIT Press, 2011.

Kurse, Kevin. *One Nation Under God: How Corporate America Invented Christian America.* New York, NY: Basic Books, 2015.

Lepler, Jessica M. *The Many Panics of 1837: People, Politics, and the Creation of a Transatlantic Financial Crisis.* New York, NY: Cambridge University Press, 2013.

Lewis, Michael. *The Big Short: Inside the Doomsday Machine.* New York, NY: W. W. Norton & Co, 2010.

Lewis, Michael. *Flash Boys: A Wall Street Revolt.* New York, NY: W. W. Norton & Company, 2014.

Lichtenstein, Nelson. *State of the Union: A Century of American Labor.* Princeton, NJ: Princeton University Press, 2013.

Link, William A. and Susannah J Link. *The Gilded Age and Progressive Era: A Documentary Reader.* West Sussex, UK: Wiley-Blackwell, 2012.

Mahar, Maggie. *Bull! What 21st Century Investors Need to Know About Financial Cycles.* New York, NY. Harper Business, 2004.

Marglin, Stephen A., and Juliet B. Schor. *The Golden Age of Capitalism*. Oxford, UK: Clarendon Press, 1991.

Mayer, Jane. *Dark Money: The Hidden History of the Billionaires behind the Rise of the Radical Right.* New York, NY: Doubleday, 2017.

McCartney, James. *America's War Machine: Vested Interests, Endless Conflicts.* New York, NY: Thomas Dunne Books, 2015.

McCartin, Joseph. *Collision Course: Ronald Reagan, the Air Traffic Controllers, and the Strike that Changed America*. New York, NY: Oxford University Press, 2011.

McKee, Thomas Hudson. *The National Conventions and Platforms of All Political Parties 1789-1905*. Sydney, New South Wales: Wentworth Press, 2016.

Moloney, Niamh; Eilís Ferran, and Jennifer Payne. *The Oxford Handbook of Financial Regulation*. New York, NY: Oxford University Press, 2015.

Morgan, Ted. *A Covert Life: Jay Lovestone: Communist, Anti-Communist, Spymaster*. New York, NY; Random House, 1999.

Muncy, Robyn. *Creating a Female Dominion in American Reform, 1890-1935*. New York, NY: Oxford University Press, 1991.

Myers, Gustavus. *History of the Great American Fortunes*. New York, NY: Modern Library, 1937.

Naim, Moises. *The End of Power. From Boardrooms to Battlefields to Churches to States, Why Being in Charge Isn't What it Used to Be.* New York, NY: Basic Books, 2013.

Nations, Scott. *A History of the United States in Five Crashes: Stock Market Meltdowns That Defined a Nation.* New York, NY: HarperCollins, 2017.

Osborne, Roger. *Civilization. A New History of the Western World.* New York, NY: Pegasus Books, 2006.

Oatley, Thomas. *International Political Economy.* Oxfordshire, UK: Routledge, 2019.

Page, Benjamin I. and Martin Gilens. *Democracy in America?: What Has Gone Wrong and What We Can Do About It.* Chicago, IL: University of Chicago Press, 2017.

Parenti, Michael. *The Assassination of Julius Cesar: A People's History of Ancient Rome.* New York, NY: The New Press, 2003.

Paul, Rand. *The Tea Party Goes to Washington.* New York, NY: Center Street, 2011.

Piketty, Thomas. *Capital in the Twenty First Century.* Cambridge, MA: Harvard University Press, 2014.

Prins, Nomi. *Collusion: How Central Bankers Rigged the World.* New York, NY: Bold Type Books, 2018.

Putnam, Robert D. *Bowling Alone. The Collapse and Revival of American Community.* New York, NY: Simon & Shuster Paperbacks, 2001.

Putnam, Robert D. *The Upswing: How America Came Together a Century Ago and How We Can Do It Again.* New York, NY: Simon & Schuster, 2020.

Raphael, Ray. *Founding Myths: Stories that Hide Our Patriotic Past.* New York, NY: The New Press, 2014.

Ratner, Sidney, and James H. Soltow, and Richard Sylla. *The Evolution of the American Economy: Growth, Welfare and Decision Making.* New York, NY: Basic Books, 1980.

Robert, Richard. *Inside International Finance. A Citizen's Guide to the World's Financial Markets, Institutions, and Key Players.* London, UK: Orion Publications, 1998.

Roberts, Alasdair. *America's First Great Depression: Economic Crisis and Political Disorder after the Panic of 1837.* Ithaca, NY: Cornell University Press, 2013.

Rothkopf, David. *Superclass: The Global Power Elite and the World They Are Making.* New York, NY: Farrar Straus and Giroux, 2008.

Sanders, Bernie. *Our Revolution: A Future to Believe In.* New York, NY: McMillan, 2016.

Schneirov, Richard. *Labor and Urban Politics: Class Conflict and the Origins of Modern Liberalism in Chicago, 1864–97.* Urbana, IL: University of Illinois Press, 1998.

Schor, Juliet B. *The Overspent American: Why We Want What We Don't Need.* New York, NY: Harper Perennial, 1999.

Schor, Juliet B. *The Overworked American: The Unexpected Decline of Leisure.* New York, NY: BasicBooks, 1993.

Simon, Rita James (edit.) *As We Saw the Thirties. Essays on Social and Political Movements of a Decade.* Urbana, IL: University of Illinois Press, 1967.

Sjursen, Daniel A. *A True History of the United States.* Lebannon, NH: Steerforth Press, 2021.

Skocpol, Theda. *Protecting Soldiers and Mothers: The Political Origins of Social Policy in the United States*. Cambridge, MA: Harvard University Press, 1992.

Stevens, Errol Wayne. *Radical L.A.: From Coxey's Army to the Watts Riots, 1894-1965*. Oklahoma, OK. Oklahoma University Press, 2009.

Stiglitz, Joseph E. *Rewriting the Rules of the American Economy: An Agenda for Growth and Shared Prosperity*. New York, NY: W. W. Norton & Company, 2015.

Stiglitz, Joseph E. *People, Power, and Profits: Progressive Capitalism for an Age of Discontent.* New York, NY: W. W. Norton & Company, 2020.

Stockman, David A. *The Great Deformation. The Corruption of Capitalism in America*. New York, NY: PublicAffairs, 2013.

Stoller, Matt. *Goliath: The 100-Year War between Monopoly Power and Democracy*. New York, NY: Simon & Shuster, 2019.

Stowell, David O. *Streets, Railroads, and the Great Strike of 1877*. Chicago, IL: The University of Chicago Press, 1999.

Strauss, William, and Neil Howe. *The Fourth Turning: An American Prophecy—What the Cycles of History Tell Us about America's Next Rendezvous with Destiny*. New York, NY: Broadway Books, 1998.

Studwell, Joe. *How Asia Works. Success and Failure in the World's Most Dynamic Region*. London, UK: Profile Books LTD, 2013.

Taibbi, Matt. *Hate Inc: Why Today's Media Makes Us Despise One Another*. New York, NY. OR Books, 2019.

Talbot, David. *The Devil's Chessboard. Allen Dulles, the CIA, and the Rise of America's Secret Government.* New York, NY: HarperCollins, 2019.

Teixeira, Ruy, and Joel Rodgers. *America's Forgotten Majority. Why the White Working Class Still Matters.* New York, NY: Basic Books, 2000.

Tepper, Johnathan, and Denise Hearn. *The Myth of Capitalism: Monopolies and the Death of Competition.* Hoboken, NJ: John Wiley & Sons, 2019.

Tirado, Linda. *Hand to Mouth. Living in Bootstrap America.* New York, NY: Putnam, 2014.

Touraine, Alain. *The Return of the Actor. Social Theory in Postindustrial Society*, Minneapolis, MI: University of Minnesota Press, 1988.

Traister, Rebecca. *All the Single Ladies: Unmarried Women and the Rise of an Independent Nation.* New York, NY: Simon & Schuster, 2016.

Tuschman, Avi. *Our Political Nature. The Evolution of What Divides Us.* Amherst, NY: Prometheus Books, 2013.

Twain, Mark. *The Gilded Age: A Tale of Today.* New York, NY: Penguin Classics, 2010.

Unger, David C. *The Emergency State, America's Pursuit of Absolute Security at All Costs.* New York, NY: The Penguin Press, 2012.

Wallerstein, Immanuel. *Historical Capitalism with Capitalist Civilization.* London, UK: Verso, 1983.

Watts, Edward J. *Mortal Republic: How Rome Fell into Tyranny*. New York, NY: Basic Books, 2018.

White, Richard D. *Kingfish: The Reign of Huey P. Long*. New York, NY: Random House, 2006.

Wilkerson, Isabel. *Caste: the Origins of Our Discontents*. New York, NY: Random House, 2020.

Wolf, Martin. *Fixing Global Finance*. New Haven, CT: Yale University Press, 2008.

Zeihan, Peter. *The Accidental Superpower.* New York, NY: Hatchet Book Group, 2014.

Zeihan, Peter. *Disunited Nations: The Scramble for Power in an Ungoverned World*. New York, NY: Harper Collins, 2020.

Zeihan, Peter. *The End of the World is Just the Beginning. Mapping the Collapse of Globalization*. New York, NY: HarperCollings, 2022.

Zevin, Alexander. *Liberalism at Large: The World According to the Economist*. New York, NY: Verso, 2019.

Zinn, Howard. *A People's History of the United States*. New York, NY: HarperCollins, 1980.

Zweig, Michael. *The Working Class Majority: America's Best Kept Secret*. Ithaca, NY: Cornell University Press, 2012.

Zweig, Michael (editor). *What's Class Got to Do with It? American Society in the Twenty-First Century*. Ithaca, NY: Cornell University Press, 2004.

APPENDICES

Appendix 1: Dramatic fall of governability

This dramatic fall in trust in governments was part of a broader, ongoing trend of declining government power and influence in the country (and in the world, too).

Government was no longer seen as the solution to the social and economic problems.

This fall in interest in political participation could be seen in the voting participation in the US, for example.

Voter turnout over the years fell during presidential elections from 66.8% in 1960, to just 54.9% in 2012.

http://www.people-press.org/2015/11/23/1-trust-in-government-1958-2015/
http://www.presidency.ucsb.edu/data/turnout.php

This trend was not just in the US. Voter participation worldwide was also declining. In 1973, for instance, worldwide voter turnout had been as high as 75%. By 2014 it had dropped to less than 65% (a 34% drop in just 44 years).

In 2015, democracy had been expected to further weaken by 26% in the Middle East and North Africa, 16% in Asia and Europe, 15% in Sub-Saharan Africa, 14% in Latin America, and

13% in North America.
http://reports.weforum.org/outlook-global-agenda-2015/
https://www.ned.org/docs/Samuel-P-Huntington-Democracy-Third-Wave.pdf
www3.weforum.org/docs/GAC14/WEF_GAC14_OutlookGlobalAgenda_Report.pdf
https://widgets.weforum.org/outlook15/05.html

Using the definition of the famous German sociologist Max Webber that says that the fundamental characteristic of a government was to claim "the monopoly of legitimate use of physical force within a given territory" to measure of the effectiveness of autocratic governments, we see here a trend that is affecting the very core function of a government, its ability to maintain this fundamental monopoly.
https://www.britannica.com/topic/state-monopoly-on-violence
https://web.stanford.edu/class/polisci211z/2.2/Arreguin-Toft%20IS%202001.pdf

Governability

Experts began wondering if governments could now continue doing what they had been created for: the governing of nations. It was a "governance" problem, it was said, a problem of "governability," both terms coined in the early 1980s, used more and more often in the Media and in academia in the later part of that same decade.
ec.europa.eu/governance/docs/doc5_fr.pdf
https://link.springer.com/chapter/10.1007/978-94-007-6107-0_2
http://sk.sagepub.com/reference/governance/n219.xml

One author even argued that the institution itself of the "nation-state" was becoming "an increasingly nostalgic fiction." An extreme statement perhaps, but one that conveyed the general concern around weakening of governments and their faltering influence.
https://assets.cambridge.org/97805218/15215/sample/9780521815215ws.pdf

The end of power?

Some argued that the decline was not just in *political* power, but also in general institutional power. Moises Naim, a Venezuelan economist (and former director of the World

Bank), argued that today the power of the military, of religious institutions, and even of corporations, were also losing strength and influence.

The problem of "governability" was, therefore, not limited to just governments, but to institutions everywhere.
See: Naim, Moises. *The End of Power. From Boardrooms to Battlefields to Churches to States, Why Being in Charge Isn't What it Used to Be.* New York, NY: Basic Books, 2013.
https://research.stlouisfed.org/publications/economic-synopses/2016/04/29/taking-stock-income-inequality-and-the-stock-market/

There was, however, a catch with this concept. Power, in general, might have been waning, including power in the business sector, as Naim claimed. But private businesses, although weakened, were not, however, losing *public approval.* In fact, they were gaining it.

Power and *public approval* are two different things, and even though business might have been losing some of their power during this period, they were not necessarily falling in their approval ratings.

In fact, trust in businesses, which had been growing since 1973, seemed to be growing. Even after the 2008 Global Financial crisis, at a time when "globalization" and "free markets" were seriously doubted by the public, at least temporarily, worldwide trust in business had, by 2016, rose to 58%. That same year, trust in governments had fallen to just 44%. Even the serious 2008 Global Financial Crisis (and the resulting Great Recession) had not changed the public's more or less growing positive view of business present since the 1980s.

Power and influence may have been waning among large businesses, just as Moises Naim argued, but *trust* in them, overall, was not receding. It was rising.

Another poll confirmed this, finding that public support for business in general had left behind all other major modern institutions (governments, churches, NGOs, and the Media, to

mention some important ones) in terms of approval rates.
https://www.edelman.com/trust2017/
https://www.edelman.com/.../2016/.../2016-Edelman-Trust-Barometer-Global-_-Lead...

Big business only began to lose again public support after 2012. Even Republicans here showed less support. Here support dropped from 75% to just 56%, a dramatic fall from grace. According to Gallup: "Republicans' dimmed views of big business coincide with a period when many Republican leaders and media personalities have publicly criticized large corporations for activism on social issues like racial justice, diversity and inclusion, and climate change."
https://news.gallup.com/poll/357755/socialism-capitalism-ratings-unchanged.aspx

Appendix 2: the problem of governance and the large banks

The problem of "governance" was evident, too, in the regulation of the economy. An attempt in 1998, for instance, by the Commodity Futures Trading Commission (a US federal agency) to impose more oversight over certain financial instruments called "derivatives" (a way to "bet" in the financial markets) was effectively ended by large US banks. Derivatives then remained unregulated for years, leading, some claim, to the 2008 Global Financial Crisis. In 1999, Congress even passed a law prohibiting any such regulation, a complete reversal of the spirit of the 1950s, when public interest came before private ones.
http://www.nytimes.com/2008/10/09/business/economy/09greenspan.html
https://www.pbs.org/wgbh/pages/frontline/warning/interviews/born.html

The banking system has been at the center of the transfer of money, so it will be useful to do a quick recapitulation of how the regulation of the financial system has varied overtime, showing shift from public to private and vice versa over the last century.

A story of bank regulation and deregulation

After the Great Depression (1929-1941), banks came under a somewhat more effective government regulation. The Banking Act of 1933, also known as the Glass-Steagall Act, had prohibited the combination of commercial and investment banking, and also saw the creation of the Federal Deposit Insurance Corporation, or FDIC, also in 1933, to protect depositors' money and to prevent "bank runs," during which depositors could lose all their money.

After 1973, however, a resurgent financial sector pressured for the reversing of banking regulations, and bring them full circle back the conditions that existed before the Great Depression. It took some time. The Glass-Steagall Act was repealed in 1999, under President Clinton, 66 years later. Some have called these kinds of changes the "Great Regression."

https://hsp.org/education/unit-plans/bank-failures-and-the-great-depression-in-philadelphia/losing-trust-in-banks
https://www.thoughtco.com/history-of-banking-reform-after-the-new-deal-1147513
https://livinghistoryfarm.org/farminginthe30s/money_08.html

Historically, the US government had always been reluctant to regulate larger banks. The government seemed to never like to face off powerful bankers, so it has traditionally left the banks to regulate themselves. This has been the overall pattern, at least since 1907: giving the banks money; hoping the problems go away.

This happened during the Panic of 1907, when the New York Stock Exchange fell almost 50%. The prominent US banker J P Morgan (1837-1913) met with other important bankers to try to stem the tide, and managed, it seemed, to have some success in limiting the impact of the Panic.

The government viewed this favorably, and Congress introduced legislation to allow larger, more "cooperative" banks, to organize themselves with the support of the

government on the condition they would assist in maintaining financial stability and act when necessary to neutralize emergencies.
http://www.u-s-history.com/pages/h952.html

The Federal Reserve System
This was the spirit behind the creation of the Federal Reserve System in 1913, America's central bank in all but name, and in charge of the country's monetary regulation, and, in time, the nation's financial stability, too (something that was added later to its goals, although its *de facto* job remains simply to protect the largest US banks).

The only time the US government ever seemed "brave" enough to curtail somewhat the banks' extraordinary influence and autonomy was in 1933, under President Franklin D. Roosevelt.

The Great Depression had led to the failure of about 9 thousand banks, the loss of 140 billion dollars in people's savings, and to unemployment rates reaching some 25%, and also damaged public trust to the point that the public supported new laws to place considerably more oversight over financial institutions.

Roosevelt's regulations, however, were not necessarily "forced" upon large banks. Banks were in agreement with separating commercial and investment because, at that point, in 1933, it would help them reestablish their own financial stability.

Furthermore, the Federal Reserve System continued in charge of the country's monetary policy, remaining a symbol of the continued autonomy and the power of large banks.

Appendix 3: The Dodd-Frank Act of 2010

A long history of compromise

Arrangements between ultra-rich banks and the government are not atypical in America. Here, these banks always enjoyed exceptional independence from the federal government.

The Federal Reserve has never been under any congressional oversight. Its chair, for instance, was appointed by the President, but its regional governors were all appointed by banks. It was, at best, a system based on compromise. *https://www.investopedia.com/articles/economics/08/federal-reserve.asp*

Appendix 4: The tax problem

Most federal revenue comes from the income and payroll taxes paid by middle-income earners. But the US is no longer a nation of middle-income earners (their percentage of the total population, as mentioned before, has already fallen below 50%, this after the 2008 Great Recession). This meant that the financial situation of the country is being significantly compromised, perhaps more so than at any time in recent history.

https://www.center-forward.org/wp-content/uploads/2012/04/Budget-Basics-Revenues-03-12-update-2.pdf

https://www.nationalpriorities.org/budget-basics/federal-budget-101/revenues/

Financial institutions are not even good forecasters. The US Federal Reserve, for instance, didn't see the 2008 crisis coming. The year before they had projected "sustainable expansion of real economic activity during the following two years," and a 2.5% expansion for 2007, and almost 3% in 2008.

https://www.federalreserve.gov/monetarypolicy/mpr_20070214_part1.htm

http://money.cnn.com/2013/01/18/news/economy/federal-reserve-transcripts/index.html

Even in 2008, already in the middle of the crisis, Fed's internal minutes showed its leaders "confounded and muddled" about the events, arguing stuff that was "patently wrong." They had, in short, a "miserable forecasting record."

https://www.forbes.com/sites/billconerly/2014/02/23/can-the-fed-stop-the-next-recession-business-cant-bank-on-it/
https://www.sprottmoney.com/blog/has-the-fed-ever-accurately-predicted-a-recession-peter-diekmeyer.html
The Feds were unaware of the severity of the crisis until at least August of 2007.
https://www.federalreserve.gov/monetarypolicy/mpr_20070214_part1.htm

The International Monetary Fund also didn't see the crisis coming. Before 2008, just as the Feds, the IMF had forecasted "robust growth for the years 2007 and 2008," with a 4.9% global expansion, and a 2.5 and 2.7% expansion for the US. The chance of a recession was very low, they said, below 3%. This now legendary error is seen as a sign of incompetence, and even studied by scholars.

www.imf.org/external/pubs/ft/weo/2007/01/pdf/text.pdf
www.frbsf.org/economic-research/files/Fri_1530_PerezQuiros_July.pdf

In truth, the forecasting of the IMF has only been "somewhat better than if they had chosen a random number."

Banerjee, Abhijit, and Esther Duflo. *Good Economics for Hard Times.* New York, NY: PublicAffairs, 2019, p. 6.

www.ingramcontent.com/pod-product-compliance
Lightning Source LLC
Chambersburg PA
CBHW051302250726
48656CB00004B/1426

* 9 7 8 1 7 2 0 2 7 3 4 8 6 *